Your Child's Emotional Health: The Early Years

Philadelphia Child Guidance Center

Your Child's Emotional Health: The Early Years

PHILADELPHIA CHILD GUIDANCE CENTER WITH JACK MAGUIRE

Produced by The Philip Lief Group, Inc.

Macmillan • USA

This book is dedicated to Margie Ouellette
and to her children,
Amanda, Carly, and Brittany.
I am proud to be a part of their family.

This book is not intended as a substitute for the professional advice of a doctor or mental health professional. The reader should regularly consult a physician or appropriate health care practitioner in matters relating to health, particularly with respect to any symptoms that may require diagnosis or medical attention.

MACMILLAN
A Prentice Hall Macmillan Company
15 Columbus Circle
New York, NY 10023

Published by arrangement with   The Philip Lief Group, Inc.
6 West 20th Street
New York, NY 10011

MACMILLAN is a registered trademark of Macmillan, Inc.

Library of Congress Cataloging-in-Publication Data
Your child's emotional health. The early years / Philadelphia Child
   Guidance Center with Jack Maguire.
        p.   cm.
   Includes index.
   ISBN 0-02-860001-0
   1. Emotions in children.   2. Emotional problems of children.
I. Maguire, Jack.   II. Philadelphia Child Guidance Center.
BF723.E6Y68   1995
649'.122—dc20   94-34151
                                                                CIP

Manufactured in the United States of America

10   9   8   7   6   5   4   3   2   1

Contents

Preface

C hildren seldom say that they need help. More often their behaviors tell us that they do. They may suffer vague, slowly evolving difficulties at home, at school, or with their peers. Or they may exhibit sudden, marked changes in their conduct and mood that pervade every aspect of their lives.

Each year, thousands of children, adolescents, and their families get help from Philadelphia Child Guidance Center (PCGC). As one of the foremost centers in the country for child and adolescent psychiatric care, PCGC offers services that are specialized and individually designed to meet the needs of each child and family. Often working in closely cooperative teams, staff members help families recognize, expand, and mobilize their strengths to make life more fulfilling for the affected child as well as for the family as a whole.

Since PCGC's origin in 1925 as one of the first centers in the world devoted to child psychiatry, it has enjoyed an international reputation for its excellent treatment and innovative research. The founding director, Frederick H. Allen, M.D., was the first board-certified child psychiatrist in the United States as well as one of the first psychiatrists to address the problems of the child in the context of the family. Within his historic thirty-year tenure, PCGC achieved a leadership position in the study and treatment of emotional problems affecting children from birth through adolescence.

Later, under the auspices of Director Salvador Minuchin, M.D., PCGC pioneered the development of structural family therapy, a systems-oriented approach that views diagnosis and treatment of a child in the context of the family and social relationships in which she or he lives. Included in that context are the child's extended family, friends, caretakers, school, and all agencies in the culture at large—social, legal, religious, recreational, and health oriented—that influence the child's life.

Today, under the clinical direction of Alberto C. Serrano, M.D., PCGC's staff of 230 professionals provides a broad range of diagnostic and therapeutic programs that directly benefit the mid-Atlantic region of the United States and serve as models for other diagnostic and therapeutic programs throughout the nation and abroad. Thanks to its strong affiliation with the University of Pennsylvania Medical School, The Children's Hospital of Philadelphia, and Children's Seashore House, PCGC is a major component of one of the most advanced health-care and health-care research centers in the country.

This books draws upon the unique experience and expertise of PCGC to offer you, as parents, practical guidelines for raising your child to be emotionally healthy. Specifically, it helps you perform the following, especially challenging activities:

■ identify and assess your child's emotional states, problems, capabilities, and needs;

■ develop an effective parenting style that best suits you and your child as individuals;

■ address the most common and most troublesome emotional difficulties that can arise in the course of your child's life;

■ ensure the emotional well-being of all family members during any emotional crisis experienced by your family as a whole or by your child individually;

■ determine if and when you, your family, and your child need professional help in managing emotional difficulties;

■ secure the professional help that is most appropriate for you, your family, and your child, according to the situation at hand.

Love for a child comes naturally to a parent and can go far toward giving a child emotional security. Parenting skills, however, are also required to meet a child's emotional needs, and they do *not* come naturally. Instead, parents must learn them.

This book is specially designed to help parents help themselves so that they in turn can help their children. Underlying everything that PCGC does—and represents—is the belief that family members have the ability to work together to solve their problems and that each family member can achieve a new and more rewarding life in the process.

Acknowledgments

Among the many people outside Philadelphia Child Guidance Center who were helpful in putting this book together, I'd like to give special thanks to Eva Weiss, to The Philip Lief Group as a whole, and to Natalie Chapman, my editor at Macmillan. Their "writer guidance" was invaluable.

Your Child's Emotional Health: The Early Years

Introduction

The human memory relies on words and language skills to identify, record, and preserve all that an individual may encounter in life. It is small wonder, therefore, that most adults have very sketchy memories of their childhood before they began school and almost no vivid memories of it before they began to speak.

The early years of life have a mysterious and elemental quality that an adult can only recapture by caring for children who are going through them. Within this special caretaking relationship, adults learn again to see the world in nonverbal ways, and they confront anew the tremendous turmoil of an existence governed so much more by raw feelings than by processed thought. It's a learning and confrontational process for adults that is not only inspiring to their lives as individuals but also vital to their effectiveness as parents.

In emotional terms, the years between birth and age six for a child are the best of times and the worst of times. Periods of paradisal bliss and security, seldom to be realized in later years, alternate wildly and unpredictably with times of unspeakable torment and despair, the likes of which are rarely, if ever, experienced by adults.

A parent is never more important to a child's physical and emotional well-being than during this time span. Therefore, it is critical that parents enter into their very young child's world single-mindedly and wholeheartedly, progressing with her or him through that world as safely and delightfully as possible.

Fortunately, the most effective aid a parent can offer a very young child is also the easiest to offer: love. In the absence of any other surety, love alone can guide both parent and child through the darkest emotional crisis. To ensure that it stands the best chance of doing so, here are three other general truths to keep in mind about the overall emotional life of children under six:

1. Every human being is born into life with a unique temperament and begins exhibiting a distinct personality right away.
The mind of a baby is not a blank slate, awaiting the impress of time and experience to produce a characteristic "self." At birth, an infant

already possesses a personal temperament, which can be defined as an innate set of tendencies to act and react in certain ways. Throughout life, this "core" temperament will determine whether she or he is basically easygoing or high-strung, tough or vulnerable, meek or bold, playful or serious, sociable or individualistic, and many other qualities that words are hopelessly clumsy in defining.

From a parent's point of view, this means remaining ever aware of the fact that a child under six is a person in her or his own right. Therefore, much of your relationship with your very young child, from the moment of birth, has to be worked out like any other that exists between two human beings: by identifying, accepting, and appreciating the similarities and differences in your respective personalities.

Your child is not mature enough—or independent enough—to meet you halfway in this process, so you'll have to be especially understanding to make up the difference. But throughout this process, you shouldn't expect your child to be just like you, nor should you feel that you are necessarily the "prime mover" of your child's behavior.

2. It's far more important simply to pay ongoing attention to children under six than it is to act or react in specific ways.

Parents of very young children are overinclined to be "doers." So much sheer physical work is required to attend to the basic needs of the child—food, sleep, clothing, shelter, cleanliness, and safety—that parents assume that a similar expenditure of effort is needed to "do something" about a child's emotional well-being.

In fact, there is much that you as a parent can do to promote and safeguard your child's emotional health, but overdoing can easily lead to emotional exhaustion for every member of the family. Your first and foremost responsibility is simply to watch over your child. This involves keeping calmly and persistently attuned to her or his moods and behaviors so that you know your child well and, consequently, when it's appropriate to be concerned.

3. Always remember that a child under six is paying especially close attention to you.

Because they are so dependent on their parents, children this young can be incredibly sensitive to how their parents feel, act, and react. Again, they mentally and emotionally process what they witness in "noncommunicable" ways that are difficult for adults to detect or appreciate.

Although your child under six may not be capable of grasping the "adult" meaning of your moods and behaviors, don't ever assume that she or he is not "old enough" to be influenced by your moods or behaviors. Be particularly mindful of how you interact with others, cope with stressful situations, or express your feelings in the presence of your very young child. The more constructively you manage your own life, the better example you will set.

Also, it's important to be honest about your moods and behaviors. Any falseness is immediately apparent and inevitably distressing to a very young child's "unsophisticated" mind. Don't lie about your feelings or actions. And don't deny—either to your child or to others in her or his presence—what your child knows to be true. Always be truthful, and it will serve both you and your child well throughout your lives together.

The information offered in this section of the book is designed to help you develop and enjoy a relationship with your very young child that nourishes her or his emotional health. Specific guidelines are organized according to the following topics:

1. SLEEPING *(Page 15)*

■ common sleeping patterns and emotional problems associated with sleeping

■ how to manage bedtime resistance, nightmares, and night terrors

■ what to do about problems associated with early rising and late sleeping

2. EATING *(Page 28)*

■ common eating patterns and emotional problems associated with eating

■ how to manage eating resistance, food fussiness, and disruptive table manners

3. SEXUALITY *(Page 31)*

■ milestones in sexual development, curiosity, and activity, and emotional issues associated with those milestones

■ how to prevent, or cope with, the sexual abuse of your very young child

■ how to minimize, or deal with, awkward sexual behavior

■ how to avoid harmful gender stereotypes in raising your child

4. SHYNESS AND AGGRESSION *(Page 43)*

■ why your child may be basically shy or aggressive and emotional problems associated with these traits

■ how to help your child cope with, and overcome, problems relating to shyness or aggression

5. FEAR *(Page 51)*

■ how fears develop in very young children; how to recognize them and how to manage them

■ a timetable of common fears at different ages

■ how to prevent, and deal with, fear associated with a hospital stay

■ at PCGC: pain management for very young children

6. DEPRESSION AND STRESS *(Page 62)*

■ causes and effects of depression and stress in very young children

■ how to prevent, manage, and overcome common problems associated with depression and stress

■ how to help your very young child remain emotionally stable through a divorce, a remarriage, a traumatic event, or a death of a loved one

7. SEPARATION ANXIETY *(Page 75)*

■ what "separation anxiety" is and why very young children experience it

■ how to cope with, and overcome, separation anxiety

8. DISCIPLINE *(Page 79)*

■ common disciplinary challenges and emotional issues associated with them; general guidelines for handling them successfully

■ how to issue commands effectively

■ how to handle the "gimmes" and the grabs when shopping with your very young child

■ how to manage whining and tantrums

■ how to evaluate and enhance your child's ability to self-discipline

14. DAY CARE *(Page 126)*

■ how day care affects the emotional health of very young children

■ how to choose and monitor day-care services

■ emotional issues relating to early education

15. PSYCHOTHERAPY *(Page 133)*

■ how to determine if your child might need psychotherapy

■ how to chose an appropriate therapy and an appropriate doctor/therapist

■ the meaning behind special diagnoses: mental retardation, autism, and attention-deficit hyperactivity disorder

■ at PCGC: preschool at-risk program

The Early Years: An Emotional Time Line

Although it is particularly difficult to define what is "normal" in the emotional life of a child under six, here are some very broad guidelines:

BIRTH TO SIX MONTHS OLD

■ becomes increasingly affectionate and demonstrative toward parents, smiling at them often and frequently responding with eagerness to facial gestures and speech

■ derives repeated joy from specific sights, sounds, and movements

■ develops ability to calm self down on certain occasions

SIX MONTHS TO ONE YEAR OLD

■ responds more and more specifically and appropriately to different types of facial gestures, speech, and interactions

■ tests environment more and more for possibly pleasurable experiences

■ develops multiple ways to initiate "love play" and to seek comfort

ONE YEAR TO EIGHTEEN MONTHS OLD

■ increasingly seeks and derives pleasure out of particular play activities

■ begins responding cooperatively and appropriately to different tones of voice (e.g., for commands)

■ develops more and more ability to control anger and dissatisfaction

■ copies behavior and emotions of others

■ seeks and develops distinct interactions with different people (especially other very young children)

EIGHTEEN MONTHS TO TWO YEARS

■ increasingly practices "pretend" games, including "pretend" emotional reactions

■ builds a repertoire of distinctly different gestures and vocalizations to express different feelings

■ occasionally seeks solitude and quiet when emotionally confused or upset

■ develops more and more ability to "read" emotional states in other people (especially parents)

■ initiates increasingly appropriate and constructive responses to other people's (especially parents') emotional states

■ works with parents to develop "codes" for communicating and managing different feelings

TWO TO THREE YEARS

■ develops ability to throw—and recover from—temper tantrums

■ increasingly initiates behavior or interactions to test emotional state—or emotional responses—of other people

■ troubles or delights self more and more with own imagination and play

■ seeks to communicate more and more feelings with specific words

■ worries more and more about the potential occurrence of distressing events

■ seeks repeated reassurance about well-being of self and family

THREE TO FOUR YEARS

■ develops increasing interest and skill in controlling emotions

■ practices "manipulating" emotions of others (especially peers)

■ starts being concerned about gender identity, modifying her or his emotional expression accordingly

■ focuses affection on parent of opposite sex, resulting in some degree of competitive antagonism toward parent of same sex

■ initiates discussions about emotional issues

■ begins exhibiting strong emotional responses—positive and negative—to dreams

FOUR TO SIX YEARS

■ seeks specific constructive outlets for emotional tension (e.g., drawing or playing particular games) in a calm and deliberate manner

■ begins making and appreciating rational judgments about causes and effects of emotions

■ becomes increasingly self-reliant in terms of pleasing self and resolving emotional disturbances

■ demonstrates more and more empathy for, and curiosity about, other people (especially peers)

■ interacts in more emotionally responsible and resilient ways with others (especially peers)

■ seeks and respects justice in emotional conflicts

At PCGC:
Early Childhood Therapy

By far the most neglected and least-defined area of psychotherapy in general involves the social-emotional problems of early childhood. Very young people are most often troubled by the same basic emotional problems that trouble adults: depression, anxiety, trauma, or grief. The manner in which such difficulties arise—or reveal themselves—in very young children tends to differ according to the following developmental stages:

THE INFANT

During infancy, social-emotional problems are interwoven with the baby's ability to regulate internal sensory processes and to make secure parental attachments. Thus, there may be "unusual" illnesses, motor-development problems, and eating or sleeping difficulties or a lack of appropriate or pleasurable responsiveness to parents.

THE TODDLER

During toddlerhood, social-emotional development is closely linked with the child's growing abilities to explore the environment, communicate, and begin individuation from her or his parents. Thus, the most common cause or effect of social-emotional problems involves some *temperamental* factor, such as an "unusual" inability to manage fear, anger, or self-control.

THE PRESCHOOLER

During the preschool years, social-emotional development is intensely involved with the increasing complexity of thought, reasoning, and communication in the child's life. Thus, the most common cause or effect of social-emotional problems involves some *cognitive* or *interpersonal* factor, such as an "unusual" lack of self-confidence, patience, or curiosity or an "unusual" amount of conflicts with, or withdrawal from, other children.

We have developed an Early Childhood Program to offer information and support to parents who are in any way concerned about their very young child's psychological development and to provide diagnostic, treatment, and outpatient services that are tailored to the needs of the individual child as well as her or his community of family members and caretakers.

With this general picture in mind, a multidisciplinary team

of professionals screens three major areas in each child's life to determine if she or he is, in fact, experiencing "unusual" social-emotional problems:

1. the child's sensory, motor, and cognitive development; temperamental characteristics; and problem-solving style

2. parental child-rearing strategies and family functioning as a whole

3. the child's relationships with other systems, such as day care, health care, and extended family networks

The program team members then use all the information and insights they have gathered to devise a specific treatment plan for the child's individual social-emotional problems. Such a plan always includes family counseling and, depending on the situation, may also feature psychosocial intervention in the child's day-care or preschool environment.

If you think that your child could benefit from this type of intervention, look for similar programs in your area.

At PCGC:
Psychological Testing
in the Early Years

Mental-health professionals, physicians, day-care workers, preschool personnel, and other specialists frequently make decisions that have a profound influence on very young children's lives. Historically, psychological testing has been a widely used and valued method for providing such professionals with the proper information to make those decisions.

Psychological testing is generally employed to determine individual differences and needs by providing specifics about a very young child's abilities, strengths, personality style, and emotional functioning. Psychological testing is also helpful in evaluating the actual or potential effects on very young children of significant situational events, such as starting kindergarten, moving to a new home, coping with a serious illness, or going through a parental divorce.

For infants and toddlers, psychological testing provides data about levels of acquisition of basic sensation-processing, motor-coordinating, communicating, learning, and adapting skills. In addition to direct observation by one or more professionals, tests that we most frequently recommend or use for these purposes are the Bayley Scales of Infant Development, the Denver Developmental Screening Test, and the Vineland Adaptive Behavioral Scales.

For preschoolers, psychological testing provides screening data about educational and intellectual levels, cognitive strengths and weaknesses, social adaptability, and school readiness. In addition to direct observation by one or more professionals, tests that PCGC most frequently recommends or uses for these purposes are the Wechsler Primary and Preschool Scale of Intelligence, the McCarthy Scales of Children's Abilities, the Stanford-Binet Intelligence Scale, and the Kaufman-ABC.

We believe that the more the family is informed about the testing and the more they are involved in the testing process, the more useful the evaluation is to them. Therefore, we employ and advocate the following testing process:

■ Before the testing begins, the psychologist (or test administrator) meets with the child and parents to identify the reasons why testing is being sought, obtain relevant background history, address any initial questions or concerns the parents have, and explain the testing process.

■ It helps to have between two and four short, separate testing sessions rather than one long one. That way, fatigue factors are minimized, and a fuller range of the child's behavior or capabilities can be observed or tested.

■ When testing is completed, the results are discussed with the family and, if appropriate, the child.

For more information about psychological testing of very young children, consult your physician or a local mental-health agency.

Psychosomatic Illness

By definition, a psychosomatic illness is a genuine physical illness that has psychological as well as biological causes (*psy-*

cho: the Greek root for mind; *soma*: the Greek root for body). More technically, such an illness is known as a *psychophysiological disorder*. As a rule, when the underlying psychological problem is effectively addressed, the physical symptoms of the illness are greatly alleviated and may disappear.

The body and the mind are so interconnected that almost any illness can be said to have a psychosomatic component. However, certain stress-sensitive illnesses are commonly thought to be especially psychosomatic in nature, such as ulcers, headaches, stomachaches, asthma, high blood pressure, and skin rashes or blemishes.

Among children in the early years, it is very difficult to determine whether a given physical illness is especially psychosomatic in nature. In part, this is due to the relatively limited manner in which they are able to verbalize their emotions or their physical sensations and needs.

Another factor complicating such a diagnosis is the tendency among children in this age range to be less inhibited about expressing their emotional problems behaviorally. Are we to infer from this proclivity that such children are *less* likely to suffer from psychosomatic illnesses because they have otherwise discharged their emotional stress? Or are we to assume that such children are *more* likely to suffer from psychosomatic illnesses because their other (i.e., behavioral) reactions to emotional stress are so strong? Who can say?

In some cases involving very young children, a particular illness may appear to be undeniably psychosomatic in nature because the behavior that it produces is so much like stress-related behavior. Nevertheless, it can't be labeled psychosomatic because no particular psychological problem can be established as a common trigger.

For example, consider *colic*, one of the more common illnesses associated with infants. Its main symptom is frequent, long-lasting crying "jags" that indicate strong physical pain, but the precise cause of this pain is maddeningly difficult to pinpoint. It may or may not be related to diet, but it is most often relieved by sustained parental attention and protection from all but the most low key and monotonous stimuli. One widely used treatment for colic is to take the baby on a long car ride so that she or he can be lulled to sleep by the nearness of the parent and the humming of the engine.

On the surface, colic appears to be a psychosomatic illness, but there is no way to tell for sure. The child whose parents are consistently very loving and attentive is just as likely to develop it as the one whose parents are consistently abusive or neglectful. And the child whose environment is consistently free of annoying, excessive, or unpredictable stimuli is just as likely to develop it as one whose environment is consistently bombarded by such stimuli.

As the parent of a very young child who suffers an illness, you need to be careful not to assume too much or too little. Whether or not a major source of your child's illness is, in fact, some emotional problem, it is always therapeutic to provide your sick child with emotional comfort and security and seek to alleviate obviously stressful conditions that she or he has recently experienced. At the same time, avoid labeling your child's illness "psychosomatic" without clear and convincing evidence (through professional consultation) that such a diagnosis is warranted. Otherwise, you may wind up subjecting yourself and your child to unwarranted guilt and responsibility.

Cognitive Development

Separate from, but interrelated with, a child's emotional development is her or his cognitive development. The expression "cognitive development" refers to a child's ability to perceive, think, and remember. As such, it is more closely associated with intellectual capabilities than with psychological makeup.

How a child feels is bound to affect how she or he perceives, thinks, and remembers—and vice versa. However, the particular cause-and-effect relationship between a child's cognitive and emotional development is dependent on many biological and social variables and differs greatly from individual to individual. Therefore, any useful picture of such a relationship in the case of a specific child can only be drawn in the context of comprehensive therapeutic treatment.

Among the many theories concerning cognitive development in children, that of the French psychologist Jean Piaget is the most popular. It divides a child's cognitive development during the early years into two distinct, age-related stages that can be described as follows:

1. Sensory-motor thinking
This stage is associated with infancy. The child acquires the ability to identify and remember different facets of the phys-

ical world (e.g., faces, sounds, toys, smells, foods). The child also learns to connect certain perceptions with particular physical actions (e.g., judging distances, moving within a given set of physical parameters, anticipating the course of simple gestures and events).

2. *Intuitive and representational thinking*

This stage is associated with toddlers and preschoolers. The child acquires language skills, recognizes major differences in individual points of view, formulates simple stories, ideas, or plans, and develops an understanding of basic time-and-space concepts.

During the middle years (ages six to thirteen), a child goes through the *concrete operations* stage of cognitive development, during which she or he develops logic and the ability to perform core intellectual activities, for example, reading, writing, computing, and experimenting. Thereafter—that is, through adolescence and adulthood—an individual is involved in the *formal-operations* stage of cognitive development, during which she or he refines intellectual capabilities and learns to conceptualize more and more philosophically.

1.
Sleeping

Popular wisdom aside, to sleep like a baby is not necessarily to do so peacefully. Natural—and individual—sleeping patterns change dramatically over the course of the first six years of life, and each new one brings with it additional challenges for both the child and the parent.

Bedtime Resistance

In the first place, there is often a big difference between a very young child's physical need to sleep and that of the family as a whole to follow a regular schedule of sleeping and wakeful periods. This difference in itself can generate all sorts of individual and interpersonal emotional crises, especially as a child matures and the *desire* to go to sleep becomes increasingly independent of the physical *need* to do so. Whether they are actually tired or not, two-year-olds who are ushered to bed before they want to be there have difficulty understanding what is happening: Are their parents punishing them? Rejecting them? Or simply incapable of appreciating how they feel?

Nightmares

In the second place, upsetting or puzzling events in a very young child's waking life are highly likely to disturb her or his sleeping life as well. People of all ages have nightmares from time to time, but they are most apparently bothersome to children between the ages of three and five, a time when they are just beginning to develop self-consciousness and vivid, self-centered fantasies. As a result, they are uniquely preoccupied, on an emotional level, with every possible threat to their success and well-being. If their fledgling powers of reason and imagination can't come to terms with a real or perceived threat during the day, then their dreams may well take it on at night.

Night Terrors

A "night terror" is an altogether different form of sleep disturbance that is especially prevalent among very young children. Characterized by eye opening, screaming, and sometimes thrashing around wildly in bed, night terrors are most commonly displayed by kids between the ages of six months to four years, usually in the early part of the night.

To the outside observer, a child experiencing a night terror seems to be reacting to an especially bad nightmare. On the contrary, brain-wave studies have shown that night terrors do not occur during dreaming periods but during the deepest levels of sleep, when mental activity is at a bare minimum. In fact, people manifesting night-terror symptoms usually remain unconscious throughout the experience regardless of whether their eyes open, their bodies move, or they speak.

Experts don't know for sure what causes a night terror, but all the evidence indicates that the source is a sudden and transitory pain or discomfort that "shocks" the child's nervous system. Frightening as it can be to the parent, a night terror is seldom symptomatic of any serious physical or psychological problem, nor does it have any lingering aftereffects. In most cases, sufferers don't even recall the experience when they wake up. However, if night terrors have a pattern of occurring more often than once every four months, it's a good idea to seek professional help.

Here is a timetable detailing the normal evolution of the three disturbances already mentioned—bedtime resistance, nightmares, and night terrors—as well as other sleep-related issues in the emotional life of a child from birth through age five:

BIRTH TO SIX MONTHS

Unless hunger, colic, illness, or pain intervenes, infants this young will typically fall asleep whenever they need to. Parents can assume that any period of wakefulness—however inappropriate it may be to an adult's daily schedule—is natural or "normal" for the child and not a sign of emotional restlessness.

SIX MONTHS TO ONE YEAR

Usually during this time span, children develop the capacity to energize themselves—or to be excited by outside stimuli—to the point where they might not fall asleep naturally. Such excitement might be triggered, or reinforced, by separation anxiety: The child either fears losing her or his parent(s) by lapsing into sleep or doesn't want to face a loss of consciousness all alone. A child may also be excited to wakefulness by a specific emotionally charged situation over which she or he has no control: for example, being put to bed in an unfamiliar room or while an exceptionally lively household occasion is still in progress.

Whatever the case, you can no longer take for granted that your child will succumb automatically to sleep whenever fatigue sets in. This is the time when you need to begin making conscious and consistent efforts to ease the transition between waking and sleeping for your child. Meanwhile, your child will probably rely more and more heavily on her or his own very helpful tension-discharging strategies, such as rocking in bed or thumb-sucking.

During this age span, children may begin experiencing night terrors, another indication that their nervous systems are much more strongly affected by outside stimuli. They may also start having nightmares; but because children this young are unable to communicate verbally, it's difficult to tell. Assuming they are capable of having a nightmare, they do not appear to be as frequently or dramatically upset by nightmares as three- to five-year-old children are.

ONE TO THREE YEARS

During these two years, children are even more susceptible to feelings that will make them want to stay awake. In addition to fearing that their parents just want to get rid of them, children start developing fears that specific things might happen to them once they are all alone in the darkness of their bedroom. Bugs might crawl over their bodies, or a monster might emerge from the closet.

Moreover, children in this age range have more detailed and retentive memories. Thus, while they're lying in bed, they begin to miss specific light-and-sound stimulations they've come to enjoy during the day. Sometimes they feel this loss so acutely, it's as if they thought that going to bed meant saying good-bye forever to their favorite pleasures.

Faced with more reasons not to go to sleep willingly, one-to-three-year-old children develop increasingly devious strategies to put off that final "good night." As communication skills get better, they progress from crying in bed to making a seemingly unending series of complaints and demands: "I don't want to," "I'm not tired," "I want a glass of water," "Give me another kiss." As powers of locomotion improve, they may go beyond merely thrashing in bed or refusing to lie down under the covers to leaving the bed altogether, either to roam around other rooms or to settle in the bed of a parent.

The variety of activities employed by an individual one- to three-year-old child to forestall sleep is usually very wide ranging. Therefore, handling bedtime resistance calls for a multifaceted, experimental response from the parent. Above all, children in this age range need help in learning to relax so that they can be both physically and emotionally ready to sleep when it's appropriate to do so.

THREE TO SIX YEARS

In general, children from three to six years old are more accepting of bedtime. They may not go to sleep right away, but they are willing to get into bed and say good night with much less fuss than when they were one to three years old. Still, occasional problems may occur.

Around the age of four, a child is sufficiently independent in spirit to appreciate having a "big" bed and an emotionally satisfying bedroom environment. Depending on the child, the latter might entail special bedclothes, reassuring pictures on the wall, and/or rearrangement of furniture that creates distinctly different areas for play, dressing, and sleep.

As indicated earlier, children from three to five are especially prone to have upsetting nightmares. It's perfectly normal during these years for them to have a nightmare as often as once or twice a week. Each specific nightmare should be taken seriously, because that approach will help the child resolve any real-life issues that caused the nightmare. However, no severe emotional disturbance is indicated unless the child has the same nightmare a number of times in close succession. In this case, you may want to consult with a professional.

The Importance of Dreaming

In 1953, researchers at the University of Chicago discovered that human beings exhibit rapid eye movement (known as REM) while they are dreaming. In other words, our eyes move around to "watch" our dreams just as they operate to see the sights of our waking life.

Following through on this discovery, sleep scientists have established that all human beings go through several dreaming cycles in the course of each night's sleep. What particularly fascinates child psychiatrists, however, is that very young children dream far more hours per day than adults, beginning with the first sleeping period after birth.

A child under the age of one dreams approximately 40 percent of fourteen sleeping hours a day, for a total daily dreaming time of 5.6 hours. By contrast, a twenty-one-year-old dreams only about 20 percent of eight daily sleeping hours, which amounts to 1.6 hours of dreaming per day.

Since normal, ongoing body functions do not take place without a life-sustaining reason, what purpose do dreams serve? And why is dreaming apparently so much more important to an infant than to an adult?

The prevailing theory is that dreams help the human mind process daily experiences and that infants have an especially strong need for this function. While dreaming, the mind plays with its emotional and conceptual faculties, testing their strengths and weaknesses against life's mysteries and ambiguities. In this manner, it maintains its own psychological health.

Infants are just starting to develop individual psyches; hence, the need for more extensive dream time. To an infant, the mental play of dreaming is especially fresh and compelling, while everything about life is mysterious and ambiguous.

Managing Nightmares

Whether or not the *cause* of a child's nightmare is a troubling issue or event in daily life, the *effect* of the nightmare all by itself can be very emotionally upsetting. When your child complains about a nightmare, here are some steps you can take to alleviate the effects of that nightmare and possibly eliminate its cause:

■ *Allow your child to wake up naturally rather than interrupting her or his sleep.*

To be jolted awake can be just as startling as the nightmare itself, and it may prevent your child's dreaming mind from reaching its own constructive "solution" to the nightmare. A nightmare that is strong enough to cause moaning and thrashing will usually provoke a child to wake up.

■ *Don't insist that the nightmare wasn't real.*

To your child, the nightmare was very real. Instead, assure your child calmly and reasonably that she or he is safe and that anything that happens in a nightmare can never really bring any harm. It may help to compare a nightmare to a television program—something that is "real" to the child but different from the way that her or his life is "real."

■ *Don't play fantasy games to get rid of the nightmare.*

If a child believes that a wicked little man is crouched under the bed, don't pretend to scare him away. As far as the child is concerned, this technique may be reassuring for the moment but not for good: The wicked little man could always return, or another wicked little man could come in his place. Instead, show the child that there *is* no such monster under the bed at that moment without either suggesting or denying that there ever *was* one under the bed.

■ *Encourage your child to describe the nightmare in as much detail as possible.*

Ask step-by-step questions about what happened in the nightmare and what your child felt as it progressed but avoid commenting or passing judgment on what your child tells you. If your child is allowed to "talk it out" without being distracted by your reactions, chances are it will lose its power to terrify. In addition, you'll learn more about how your child's dreaming imagination works, what scares your child, and, possibly, what may have triggered the nightmare in the first place.

■ *Ask your child to draw a picture of what was scary in the nightmare.*

Like "talking out" a nightmare, this activity enables your child to externalize scary images, thereby rendering them less threatening.

■ *Ask your child to describe what she or he could do to make things better if the same experience were to occur again.*

This request induces your child to rehearse coping strategies, both consciously and subconsciously, that will help her or him manage this specific type of nightmare, if it recurs, as well as similarly upsetting nightmares and real-life situations.

■ *Take appropriate measures to make your child feel more emotionally secure at night.*

If your very young child is afraid of falling asleep because of the possibility of a nightmare, the result can be a physically and emotionally harmful pattern of sleeplessness. To prevent this, it makes sense to foster a greater sense of security by leaving the bedroom door ajar or a night-light on or playing a radio softly. If your child wakes up from a nightmare and is especially upset, consider letting her or him sleep the rest of that night with you.

Managing Night Terrors

■ *Don't expect that your child can hear you or even sense your presence.*

A child in the throes of a night terror is still deeply asleep, even if her or his eyes are open and she or he is screaming, talking, and/or moving around. Indeed, the strongest indication that a child is having a night terror instead of an unusually severe nightmare is that she or he doesn't respond appropriately to outside stimuli even though she or he appears awake. Thus, your child may be screaming, "Mommy, Mommy, where are you?" while you are holding her or him in your arms.

■ *Don't wake up your child unless absolutely necessary.*

Typically, an episode of night terror lasts only a few moments, and the child returns to a normal sleeping pattern with no ill effect. Therefore, to avoid escalating the child's panic, it's best to let it run its course rather than waking the child.

If you hold your child, be gentle and don't resist any strong efforts to break free. Remember, your child doesn't realize that you are there. If your child gets out of bed and moves around, follow her or him and do what you can to prevent accidents. Assuming you are physically strong enough and meet with no resistance, pick your child up and carry her or him back to bed.

An exception to the "don't wake up" rule: anytime your child's movements threaten to result in injury. When this happens, you should definitely rouse the child to wakefulness, but do so gently. If possible, try waking your child by wiping her or his face with a washcloth soaked in warm water.

■ *Don't expect your child to remember having a night terror after awakening.*

To keep from worrying your child unnecessarily, it's best not to mention the episode at all unless she or he brings it up. The latter sometimes happens when the child awakens during the night terror itself. In any event, your response to the incident should be calm rather than concerned.

Managing Bedtime Resistance

There are two main schools of thought regarding how to handle a toddler (one to three years old) who cries instead of going to sleep:

1. Assuming the toddler isn't genuinely hungry or in pain, let her or him cry. Difficult as it is to ignore a crying child, you should recognize that she or he is simply releasing tension—something that everyone must learn for oneself and that the child will eventually become better at.

2. Go to the toddler and stay in the room, while performing some soothing activity, until she or he has calmed down. Then leave the room. Over time, the toddler's fears regarding bedtime will disappear.

In practice, individual mothers and fathers must experiment with both schools of thought and arrive at a compromise strategy that works not only for their child but also for them.

Generally, toddlers respond best if there is a regular going-to-bed routine that offers a gradual release from you and the day. When you put a one-year-old to bed, try staying in the room for a while, reading or performing some other relatively quiet activity by yourself. Month by month, spend less and less time in the room after you've said good night.

As soon as a child begins to talk, crying as a sleep-resisting activity gradually gives way to calculated defiance and manipulation. To prevent this or to keep it within manageable limits, regular going-to-bed routines assume even more importance.

Having a good routine isn't necessarily a matter of sticking to the same *bedtime* every night. While an overall consistency in bedtime is helpful, a child is not always tired at the same time night after night, nor does the same routine bedtime always suit the family schedule. Instead, having a good routine means preserving the same basic bedtime *ritual* every night, one that creates a peaceful, reassuring transition between waking and sleeping. Here are some suggestions:

■ *Let your child know when it's time to get ready to go to bed.*

Give ten or fifteen minutes' notice *ahead* of the time when your child is expected to be in bed. This will enable your child not only to do something, or finish doing something, before bedtime but also to get into a "bedtime" frame of mine.

■ *Make sure anything your child may need during the night is within reach of her or his bed.*

Children often put off falling asleep by asking for things they "need": a glass of water, a favorite toy, a tissue. Anticipate such needs and keep the area around the bed well stocked.

■ *Help your child follow a definite sequence of activities before retiring.*

In addition to using the bathroom and undressing, these activities might include putting playthings away, saying good night to family members and pets, and arranging stuffed animals on the bed for sleep.

■ *Give going to bed a ceremonial quality.*

For example, while you and your child walk into the bedroom together, sing a certain song together only at that time. Or light a candle after your child gets under the covers and blow it out after you've said your final good night. Such ceremonial touches influence children to take bedtime more seriously.

■ *Do something special with your child after she or he is tucked in for the night.*

Telling or reading stories is the ideal activity because it works the best to pacify your child. But you can also play quiet games or talk about what happened that day. There should be a well-defined pattern to whatever you do together so that the session can begin and end in a predictable, easy manner. If you tell stories, set a limit of no more than two stories. If you play a game, the game should have a built-in ending. If you talk about what happened that day, structure the conversation according to a certain fixed pattern of questions (e.g., ending a talk about the day with the question "What did you do right before you came to bed?" [answer], and "What are you going to do now?").

■ *Follow a definite rule about saying good night.*

When it's time for your child to be left alone to sleep, say good night in a prearranged, "inviolable" way (e.g., "Night, night until tomorrow"). Stick to this final declaration as much as possible, appealing to the fact that you've already said your special "good night" if your child tries to prolong bedtime.

Managing Early and Late Risers

Getting the day off to a good start is just as vital to a very young child's psychological health as ending it well. Many children routinely wake up much earlier—or later—than their parents. In most cases, this is not a symptom that the child is getting more or less sleep than necessary or that she or he is suffering from some sort of sleep-disturbing emotional problem. Nevertheless, it can create havoc within the family, which will inevitably wind up stressing the nervous systems of parent and child alike.

If your very young child is an early or late riser, first find out whether there are grounds for being concerned about her or his physical or emotional well-being. Monitor sleeping and waking patterns closely for a couple of weeks. A child who sleeps about the same number of hours each night, wakes up in a good mood, and doesn't appear to tire easily during the day is probably getting all the sleep necessary and is not suffering from a sleep-disturbing physical or emotional problem.

Next, take whatever action you can to help your child stay in bed longer or rise earlier, depending on which course of action is necessary for the family as a whole to function effectively. Patience and limited expectations are essential: It's very difficult to change a child's natural inclination to get out of bed or stay in it, especially if she or he is between one and a half and two years old.

GUIDELINES FOR EARLY RISERS

■ *Don't try putting your child to bed later in hopes that she or he will sleep longer as a result.*

This technique usually doesn't work; and even if it does, it's not worth the possible ill effects of tampering with your child's normal bedtime.

■ *Talk to your child firmly and responsibly about the issue.*

Tell your child to stay in bed without disturbing you until you come to get her or him. Reassure your child that you will not let her or him sleep "too long." (Children sometimes fear having done so when they first wake up.)

■ *Give your child suggestions and rehearsals for falling back to sleep.*

Make "falling back to sleep" a more fun thing to do for your child. Explain and demonstrate how to lie quietly, how to keep one's eyes closed, and how to think of peaceful things so that falling back to sleep can be more easily accomplished.

■ *Outfit your child's bedside with toys, water, and a little food.*

If given the chance, young children are capable of entertaining themselves and satisfying their simple hunger and thirst needs. Increase the odds that they will do this upon awakening by making it more convenient for them. Place quiet toys, a glass of water, and/or some simple crackers (such as graham crackers) within reach of the bed.

■ *Reinforce positive behavior with praise.*

Congratulate your child whenever she or he stays in bed and doesn't disturb you.

GUIDELINES FOR LATE RISERS

■ *Don't try putting your child to bed earlier in hopes that she or he will rise earlier as a result.*

It's unlikely to work, and interfering with your child's normal bedtime may only create yet another problem.

■ *Talk to your child firmly and responsibly about the issue.*

Tell your child that getting out of bed earlier will allow you to begin the day together in a better way. Ask her or him what each of you could do to help achieve this goal.

■ *Make early morning as pleasant as possible for your child.*

If your child can anticipate a few moments of play with you upon awakening or a special breakfast treat, she or he may eventually take the initiative to get up earlier.

■ *Suggest and rehearse behaviors that will make waking up easier.*

Practice simple stretching exercises with your child and give her or him simple phrases to speak that will make waking up more successful and enjoyable. For example, show your child how to take turns stretching each arm and leg in a particular sequence while saying, "I'm going to have a great day today."

■ *Try waking your child with your voice before rousing her or him physically.*

Children need to become responsible for waking themselves. If you consistently shake your child awake, the process is postponed. If, instead, you awaken your child with a soft voice, she or he must still make an independent effort to come to full consciousness.

One note of caution: Observe your child closely before disturbing her or his sleep. If you notice rapid eye movement under the eyelids, your child is dreaming, and it's less emotionally jarring for the child to remain asleep until dreaming has stopped.

Above all, don't yell. It's far too disruptive to your child, to you, and to anyone else within earshot. If a soft voice won't do the job, it's better to proceed to gentle physical arousal.

■ *Try giving your child an alarm clock.*

If your child persists in sleeping late and nothing works but physical arousal, you might want to try an alarm clock. To underscore the importance of this step to both of you, you can go together to buy the clock and then show your child how to use it. This will make your child much more responsible for her or his awakening, which should help matters considerably.

■ *Reinforce positive behavior with praise.*
Every time your child gets up at an appropriate time for the family, offer your admiration and thanks.

CASE:

Shedding Light

Eight-month-old Kelly cried every night after she was put to bed. Her parents had installed a night-light in her bedroom, but it didn't seem to help much. Kelly still started crying the instant her mother or father switched off the main light.

One night, as Kelly's father was carrying her into the bedroom, Kelly reached out her hand toward the light switch. Her father carried her over to the switch and let her play with it for a while, turning it off and on. That night, for the first time in many nights, Kelly didn't cry when her father switched off the light. Thereafter, it was a rare night when she did cry.

What a very young child doesn't know can hurt him or her emotionally. Even a small piece of knowledge given to a brain starving for knowledge can have a strong and positive impact.

2.

Eating

So much attention today is focused on getting children to eat the right things that much more common and potentially more serious issues are obscured: getting children to eat at all and getting them to eat in a manner that isn't emotionally upsetting to them and the people around them. While children under six years old seldom suffer from major eating disorders with psychological roots—such as self-imposed starvation (anorexia) or deliberate binging (bulimia)—they commonly experience a wide range of problems in coming to terms with the eating schedules, diets, and contexts that are imposed on them by the outside world.

Each child has a unique set of idiosyncratic eating tastes and habits. Consequently, experts have difficulty making general statements about what is normal for very young children, when it is appropriate to expect problems, or how to go about dealing with troublesome situations.

The first year of a child's life tends to go relatively smoothly as far as eating is concerned. The child eats heartily, if messily, and usually doesn't seem upset during feeding times (except sometimes when there is a greater-than-normal amount of distraction in the immediate environment, such as during a large family dinner).

Problems such as consistently being finicky about certain foods, refusing to eat, or misbehaving while eating—all of which are closely related—rarely develop before age two, at which point children have gone through a natural reduction in their appetite. Most often, such problems do not become seriously bothersome until the child is age three or older.

If your child exhibits one of these eating problems, the first and foremost guideline is not to worry unnecessarily about whether she or he is getting the "proper" nutritional input, especially if she or he gives every other indication of being healthy. Keep close track of what your child eats over a week's time, consult with your pediatrician, and accept the latter's judgment. Then experiment with these suggestions, depending on the specific nature of your child's problem:

■*Be as patient as possible and avoid making a big deal out of your child's poor eating habits.*

Remember that time heals many bad eating habits of children this young and that any extra attention associated with their poor eating habits—even negative attention—can reinforce those habits.

■*Make mealtimes as calm and as free from competing stimuli as possible.*

Try feeding your child alone, away from others. She or he shouldn't eat with older children and adults until ready to do so. Provide plenty of time and space to eat but don't let mealtime drag on longer than thirty minutes at the most. Your child needs to learn to take advantage of eating times while they last.

■*Note what times of day and under what circumstances your child eats best and try to arrange mealtimes accordingly.*

You may find out that your child eats best when you're in the proper mood to serve a meal, when no one else is home, or just after you've played with or washed her or him.

■*If your child must join the rest of the family for a meal, avoid arguments and problematic situations.*

Don't insist that your child eat certain foods, eat in a certain way, or display certain table manners. Also, don't expect to eat your own meal undisturbed by your child!

Follow your child's lead and allow whatever behavior least interferes with the rest of the family. Also, try to prevent or downplay arguments between you and other family members over your child's behavior at the table. They can only lead to a more stressful mealtime for everyone.

■*Don't offer your child food between meals.*

Get your child to accept the fact that there are certain times when it is more appropriate than others to eat, since doing so requires your cooperation.

■*Introduce new foods singly and in a pleasant, low-key manner.*

Don't make a big fuss over new foods. In fact, try at first to present them to your child without making any comment whatsoever. Remember that children over two years old appreciate an attractive presentation. Food doesn't have to be offered in a gourmet manner, but nice eating utensils and pleasant-looking portions can make a difference in getting the child to start eating.

■ *Don't force your child to eat when she or he won't.*

You can make several calm efforts to try to persuade your child to eat; but don't override a final no by shoving food into your child's mouth. This can only aggravate an eating problem.

■ *If your child repeatedly refuses to eat or consumes what you perceive to be too little, serve small portions of what your child likes best.*

First, do whatever you can, following your child's lead, to get your child to eat and enjoy the food in an acceptable manner. Once this goal is accomplished, you can pay more attention to *what* is eaten.

■ *Do not offer your child a highly desired item with little nutritional value until she or he eats at least a small amount of a more nutritional food.*

This is a time-honored technique that can be very effective with most children. Just be careful not to abuse it. Save it for especially important times; and while you should always stick to your bargain, you should do so in a calm, matter-of-fact manner, without theatrics.

■ *Don't worry very much about table manners until other, more significant problems have been overcome.*

Acquiring good table manners is a fairly sophisticated skill. You can't expect too much until your child is around seven or eight and has learned through increased socialization that manners in general are important. Make your child aware of what good table manners are— and encourage any effort made to develop them—but don't insist that your child display good manners against her or his will.

■ *If you can't help being concerned about your child's eating habits, by all means consult your pediatrician.*

It's better to be safe than sorry. Rely on your pediatrician's judgment about whether the problem is emotional in nature and, therefore, whether to consult a child psychologist or psychiatrist.

3.

Sexuality

Few things are more difficult for an adult to appreciate than the sexuality of a very young child. Once the major hormonal changes of puberty have begun, sexual feelings are irrevocably imbued with eroticism—the drive to have physical union with another person. Thus, in the adult world, sexuality turns into a moral issue, with countless individual and social distinctions between what is good and what is bad, what is acceptable and what is not. To a very young child, however, sexual feelings are not erotic; they simply provide sensory pleasure. And rather than compelling a child to mate with another person or reconcile all sorts of complicated emotional reactions, they merely inspire curiosity.

In the evolution of a human being, sexuality first manifests itself as an instinctive response to physical stimulation. The genitalia themselves may not be the initial target of stimulation, but they wind up registering that stimulation; and this response cycle begins much earlier than is commonly realized.

Ultrasound photography has shown that males have erections even before birth; and although ultrasound photography is not yet capable of observing the female fetus's genitalia as closely, there's every reason to infer that females experience prebirth sexual stimulation as well. Shortly after birth, both males and females have shown that they are physiologically capable of achieving orgasm.

Infants can trigger their own sexual feelings by kicking, rocking, or rubbing against their clothes; or sexual feelings can be triggered in infants when their bodies are touched, caressed, and lulled by their parents and caretakers. As infants mature into toddlers, many of their favorite activities can produce sexual pleasure as a side effect: jumping, bouncing, wrestling, sliding, swinging, and seesawing.

Eventually, toddlers start responding to sexually charged images and situations that exist in their environment. Around age two, children begin exhibiting a keen interest in parts of the body—not just their own but that of others as well, especially those that have a different type of genitalia. Children from age two to five also like to mimic the sexual nuances of adult behavior that they see at home, on television, or in printed matter. They playfully undress themselves, assume provocative poses, or make flirtatious body movements.

Aside from the personal embarrassment such activities may cause you, particularly if they occur in public, they are harmless and unlikely to preoccupy a child's attention for more than a moment or two at a time. It may be appropriate in certain situations for you to help your child control or discontinue a specific act of sexual behavior; but if you make too big an issue of such behavior, you may inhibit your child's early sexual learning, which may result in sexual problems later in life.

On a more positive level, there are ways in which you can help a very young child—even as young as two years old—respect and enjoy her or his sexuality. That male genitals are much more visible than female sexual organs can cause very young children of either sex a considerable amount of worry. Girls may need to be convinced that their bodies are just as beautiful and as marvelously equipped as male bodies. Boys may need to be reassured that their penises will not fall off (an anxiety that can lead to frequent masturbatory "double checks"). Both boys and girls need to be told, in a general way, *how* their genitalia will change as they grow older so that they won't jump to distressing conclusions.

By the age of three, a child usually begins forming a romantic attachment to the parent of the opposite sex (or, lacking this person, to some other adult of the opposite sex or to adult members of the opposite sex in general). In doing so, the child is not motivated by erotic feelings but by social and psychological forces.

In their eagerness to express their freshly appreciated gender identity, three-year-olds are compelled to imitate the male and female relationships that they observe in the adult world. Girls will compete with mother for father's attention; boys will compete with father for mother's attention. It's an ebbing-and-flowing process that usually peaks around age six but can continue for another year or two. By age eight, a child typically seeks self-expression through a more direct and mature identification with the parent of the same sex.

During these turbulent years when a child's interest and affections are increasingly focused on the parent of the opposite sex, there is little that parents can do except to be patient and understanding. Girls should be given more time alone with their fathers—and boys, with their mothers—provided it doesn't interfere unduly with the amount of time that mothers and fathers need to be alone together. As children are taught that their own rights will be respected by their parents, they should also be taught to respect their parents' rights.

It's not unusual for children in this age range to strike out at the "competitive" parent. For example, a very young daughter may be quick to scream "I hate you!" at her mother anytime her mother does something disagreeable, especially whenever her mother thwarts her efforts to claim her father's exclusive attention. In such a case, the rejected parent should not take the outburst personally. It is the parent's role, not the parent as an individual, that the child finds so intolerable.

If you are verbally abused in this way, bear in mind that very young children are just learning to master their emotions as well as their language skills. Therefore, what they impulsively blurt out in a moment of strong emotion is very likely to be crude and misleading. Don't reinforce such behavior by saying something like "It hurts me to hear you say that" or "I don't like you very much, either, when you say nasty things." Remain calm and let your child know that you still love her or him.

Another less extreme but no less upsetting form of rejection-behavior is for the frustrated child to avoid contact with the rival parent or to express consistently a preference to be with the parent of the opposite sex. Again, the best strategy is to remain calm and allow the child to do as she or he wishes, assuming it doesn't create any undue complications. Assure the child that it's okay with you if she or he would rather be with the other parent but that you'd like to spend time together later.

It's perfectly normal for a phase of repeated verbal abuse or avoidance to last as long as a month. If the behavior persists at the same level of intensity for more than a month, then there may be an underlying problem—such as a stressful situation within the family (e.g., marital discord, an impending birth, or an exceptional disruption of normal routine)—that is aggravating the child's relationship with the parent she or he is rejecting. If you think that there may be a specific reason that your child is so consistently manipulating one parent against another, then it may be wise to consult with a child psychiatrist or psychologist to find out how best to manage the problem.

As for sex education in general, it is never too early to begin. In fact, the earlier you start, the easier it is. As a child grows older, the significance of sex becomes increasingly more complicated. Therefore, take immediate and appropriate advantage of any opportunity your child gives you to talk about sexual matters, such as a question related to sex or some behavior that manifests her or his sexuality.

In conversations with your very young child about sex, be direct. Talk to your child in the particular manner that you and your child have developed for discussing interesting subjects. And avoid misnaming parts of the body or inventing "short-cut" fantasy explanations for sexual processes. These cover-up strategies can create unnecessary and even harmful confusion and embarrassment later. For example, a child told that a baby grows in the mother's stomach may actually become nervous about what she or he eats.

In any type of educational endeavor, preparation is all-important. The sex-related questions most commonly posed by a child between the ages of two and six are as follows:

Why don't I have a penis? Breasts? Genital hair?

Where do babies come from? Can I have a baby?

What does "[sex-related term or expletive]" mean?

Anticipate such questions and any others that you feel your child may ask. Then prepare ways to answer them truthfully, in the manner that's most comfortable to you, that's most likely to satisfy your child's natural curiosity, and that teaches your child to associate sexuality with personal responsibility.

For example, in answer to your daughter's question about why she doesn't have a penis, you may want to say simply, "Because you're a girl, you have a vagina instead of a penis. Boys don't have a vagina. A vagina is a private part of a girl that is just as special as a penis is for a boy." In answer to your child's question "Can I have a baby?," you may want to say, "No, your body has to grow up more before you can have a baby. And it takes two grown-up people to make a baby— a man and a woman. The best way for them to have a baby is when they are in love and want to stay together to raise their baby in a family."

Sexual Abuse of the Very Young

Tragically, children of *any* age can be victims of sexual abuse. The abuser of a child age six or under is most likely to be someone who is in frequent contact with the child—a family member, a relative, a friend, a neighbor, or a caretaker, who may consider the abuse itself a harmless bit of fun, even an act of love. Nevertheless, it is an outrageous violation of the child's privacy and emotional well-being, and it can easily turn physically dangerous as well.

No matter how young the victim of sexual abuse is, the long-term psychological damage is potentially horrible. Assuming the abuse is not painful, a child-victim under six years old probably won't regard the sexual activity as "wrong" but will certainly be puzzled about how such an experience factors into intimate relationships with others. If the abuse occurs repeatedly (which is more likely than not in cases involving children), a victim this young will be totally unable to deal with the overstimulation and will eventually intuit from the abuser that something strange and bad is going on. If the child tries to end the abusive behavior, the abuser might resort to emotional or even physical retaliation.

To help prevent child abuse, make sure very young children understand that if anyone touches them and makes them feel "funny," they should first tell the person to stop and then come to you and let you know what has happened. Also, you should avoid using exaggerated language when you advise children to respect adults. For example, don't say to a very young child, "Always do what the baby-sitter says."

If you suspect that your very young child has been sexually abused, look for physical evidence in a routine manner that won't scare the child. Although it's difficult to detect behavioral signs of sexual abuse, be alert to the possibility of abuse if your child does any of the following:

■ exhibits an unusual degree of preoccupation with sexual matters or with her or his genital area;

■ communicates aspects of sexual abuse in drawings, games, or fantasies (e.g., pictures of a larger figure molesting a smaller figure or doll play involving sexual seduction);

■ displays a radical change in behavior, especially involving fear, anger, or withdrawal in regard to a specific individual, situation, or place.

If your child offers any hint that sexual abuse has occurred, calmly encourage her or him to talk freely, without making any judgmental comments. Don't refute what your child says or react with astonishment. Take everything your child says seriously and assure her or him that telling you was the right thing to do. (Abusers often swear their victims to secrecy and threaten them with punishment for disclosure.) Finally, tell your child that you will take action to make sure that he or she is safe and that the abuse won't happen again.

If the suspected abuse has occurred *within* the family, immediately contact your local Child Protection Agency. If the suspected abuse has occurred *outside* the family, immediately contact your local police department or district attorney's office. Anyone reporting to these agencies in good faith is immune from prosecution. These agencies will advise you about what steps you should take, given the situation. Among the recommended steps will almost certainly be consulting with a pediatrician and a child psychologist or psychiatrist.

Managing Awkward Sexual Behavior

PUBLIC REMARKS OR DISPLAYS

There will inevitably be times when your very young child will embarrass you with remarks or displays of a sexual nature while the two of you are among other adults inside or outside your home. Perhaps the mere presence of other physically mature sexual beings excites your child to behave in this manner. Maybe your child instinctively knows that the best time to indulge in this kind of behavior is when others are around to temper your reaction. Most likely your child has just unwittingly chosen to do something perfectly natural at the wrong time.

If your child asks you a question about sex where other people can overhear you, don't betray your discomfort or frustrate your child's healthy curiosity by saying that you'll answer the question later. Instead, answer the question briefly in general terms and try to lead the conversation elsewhere.

If your child undresses in public, resist the impulse to scold. Instead, take your child gently aside (if possible), quietly explain that there's a rule people follow about keeping their clothes on in public, and say that you want her or him to remain dressed when other people are around.

If your child calls attention to someone else's sexual characteristics in a voice loud enough to be overheard, the same basic strategy applies, with an added appeal to the child's innate capacity for empathy. Take your child gently aside (if possible), quietly explain that other people feel uncomfortable when they hear someone talking about them, and say that you don't want her or him to behave in such a way.

SEXUAL GAMES

Beginning around age two and a half and continuing until around age seven, most children remain ever eager to explore similarities and differences in physical sexual characteristics with their peers. As with any venture into the unknown, they tend to conduct this activity in the safely structured context of a game—either "show," in which the participants take relatively formal turns exhibiting their genitals in an agreed-upon manner; "house," in which the participants imitate mother and father by getting naked in front of each other; or "doctor," in which the participants "scientifically" investigate each other's genitals.

Children in this age group who engage in sexual games are motivated by intellectual curiosity, not erotic drive, and so their exploration seldom progresses beyond observing each other, nor does it feature any of the emotional give-and-take associated with romantic love. From a psychological point of view, the greatest potential danger of such sexual play to the participating child lies in the way in which an adult witness handles the situation. If an adult's direct intervention or follow-up is too strong, abrupt, or disapproving, the child is bound to experience a mixture of confusion, embarrassment, shame, and guilt that she or he will subconsciously attach to sexual matters in general.

Whenever you interrupt children in the middle of sexual games, do so gently. Explain to the children that a body is something private and that they should keep their clothes on when they play together. Whenever you are compelled, after the fact, to talk to your child about sexual play, first ask your child what she or he did, then offer the "privacy" explanation and the "keep your clothes on" guideline.

MASTURBATION

Masturbation is a natural way for a very young child to explore and enjoy her or his sexuality. At this stage of life, it consists of a wide progression of activities building in intensity, from tentatively crossing the legs or rubbing the genitals while fully clothed to undressing and vigorously fondling the genitals.

Because masturbation represents a healthy activity for the very young child, your goal in managing your child's masturbatory habit should not be to prohibit it but, rather, to get her or him to regard it as a personal activity that should be performed only when alone. Whenever you observe your very young child doing what you suspect is masturbating, first find out in a casual, nonthreatening way if masturbation is, in fact, what is going on. If you haven't already identified it to your child as "the private thing," then ask your child if the activity is making her or his genitals feel good. Once you've established that your child is masturbating, identify and explain it as "the private thing."

INTRUSION ON PARENTAL SEXUAL ACTIVITY

Disconcerting as it can be for your child to appear unexpectedly when you're having sexual relations, try to remain as composed as possible. First tell your child that you are enjoying your "private time" now. ("Enjoy" is an important word, since it may appear to your child that you're being hurt or bothered.) Then ask your child to leave you alone for a while, with the assurance that you will spend time together later. Of course, the most effective strategy is to anticipate such an intrusion and take measures (such as locking the door) so that you won't be interrupted.

QUESTIONS AND ANSWERS

Gender Stereotypes

■ *Are there any innate differences in emotional makeup between males and females?*

It is virtually impossible to prove that a child's gender in itself predetermines anything about her or his emotional makeup. However, recent scientific studies suggest that females do have a stronger inborn tendency toward empathy and altruism than males.

For example, it's been repeatedly demonstrated that newborn females are quicker to cry in response to another infant's cry than are newborn males and that girls under five years old try more often and more earnestly than their male counterparts to come to their mother's aid when she seems troubled. Moreover, females of *all* ages have been shown to be more adept than males at interpreting emotional states in other people. (Most tests of this nature involve responding to photographs of people expressing strong emotions that are already known to the test administrator.)

Perhaps evolution has favored this trait in women as a mothering skill or as a means of surviving among physically stronger men. Whatever the case, there is no other scientific indication of any difference in innate emotional makeup between males and females.

■ How do parents commonly tend to stereotype emotional differences between very young boys and very young girls?

In stereotypical terms, very young boys are regarded as being emotionally stronger and less complex than their female counterparts. Therefore, parents in general are likely to treat very young girls far more delicately and sensitively than they do very young boys.

If a girl under the age of six does something naughty, she typically receives a mild rebuke and a careful explanation of what was wrong with her behavior. If a boy under six does the same thing, the punishment is typically harsher and the explanation (if any) more superficial.

In expressing affection to children in this age range, parents are usually more effusive in their language and gestures with girls than they are with boys. Moreover, in giving commands, parents are inclined to be more circumspect with girls than with boys. Assuming, for instance, that a father wants his daughter to join him, he tends to couch the command in relatively polite language: "Sweetheart, would you come over to Daddy, please?" Assuming that the same father wants his son to join him, he tends to be more abrupt: "Son, come over here."

In reality, there is no scientific basis whatsoever for believing that males are inherently stronger and less complex in their *emotional* makeup than females. (That boys seem to be more inclined toward rough *physical* behavior is a different issue.) Nor is there any logic to support a particular mode of parental treatment as intrinsically better for one sex than the other.

■ How can gender stereotyping harm young children emotionally?

Anytime you think of, or act toward, someone in a stereotypical manner—or influence another to react similarly—you are denying her or his unique identity as a human being, and any such denial can be emotionally frustrating to the victim.

This is just as important to remember when that "someone" is a very young child as it is when dealing with a fully grown adult.

It's humanly impossible to be 100 percent "correct"—that is, nonstereotypical—in your thinking and behavior. However, as a general rule, you should strive to treat a child according to her or his individual personality and not according to how you think "a little boy" or "a little girl" *should* be treated.

■ *How can parents fight against gender stereotyping in the world and raise emotionally well balanced children?*

Gender stereotyping usually begins at birth. If the infant is male, the socially approved color for clothes and playthings is a cool blue, and the appropriate decorative motifs include wild animals, sports equipment, and streamlined stripes or checks. If the infant is female, the color is a soft pink, and the motifs include kittens, flowers, and luxuriant frills.

These distinctions imply major differences between very young males and females; but as far as the children themselves are concerned, there are no apparent differences in feeling or behavior for years to come. Until children are around three or four years old, parents can effectively combat gender stereotyping simply by being careful not to treat a little girl as if she were different from a little boy and vice versa. This means not only resisting the tendency to cooperate with artificial gender distinctions in clothing and playthings but also giving a child of either gender the same kind of attention and care.

When children reach the age of four or five, they begin responding on their own to the gender stereotypes they see everywhere in the world around them, and parental efforts to fight against these stereotypes become much more problematic. On the one hand, it is impossible to deny that male and female stereotypes exist and that they have a major influence on human affairs and relationships. On the other hand, children are naturally and irresistibly drawn to enact such stereotypes in order to bolster the newly emerging sense of who they are.

The best that you can do to fight gender stereotypes at this stage in your child's life is to continue setting a good example. As much as possible, try to behave the same way toward male as you do toward female children and guard against stereotypical gender behavior in your own adult life. In two-parent households, the more fathers and mothers share the same child-raising responsibilities, the better. In one-parent households, it helps to make sure that the child has one special adult of the opposite sex with whom she or he can interact on a regular and frequent basis.

Meanwhile, allow your child to experiment with stereotypical gender roles as she or he wishes. It doesn't do much good to give your four-year-old son a doll if he'd rather have a dump truck or to pressure your five-year-old daughter to play baseball with the boys if she'd prefer to bake cookies with the girls. However, it can do a lot of good to expose your daughter or son to a wide range of different toys and activities, regardless of male and female stereotypes, and to avoid encouraging stereotypical gender behavior at the expense of giving your child full freedom of choice.

If your child's stereotypical behavior is injurious to someone else emotionally or physically, you should intervene as constructively as possible to help her or him appreciate the nature of the offense. For example, if you witness your five-year-old daughter striking a male playmate and then taunting him by saying, "Boys can't hit girls," you should immediately tell her that people shouldn't hit each other at all, regardless of whether they are boys or girls.

The Oedipus/Electra Complex

According to Sigmund Freud, a child between the ages of four and six typically experiences an intense romantic attraction to the parent of the opposite sex (or, in the absence of this parent, to some other adult of the opposite sex who plays a major role in her or his life). In response to this powerful attraction, the child also experiences a strong feeling of competitiveness and even anger toward the parent of the same sex (or toward any adult interested in—or involved with—the love object).

In the case of boys, Freud called this phenomenon an Oedipus complex, after the legendary Greek hero and supposed orphan who unknowingly killed his father and married his mother. In the case of girls, he called it an Electra complex, after the daughter of the Greek king Agamemnon, who killed her mother out of obsessive love for her father. These Greek myths are to be taken not as *literal* portrayals of a real child's possible feelings for her or his parents but, rather, as *symbolic* exaggerations of the passionate, mysterious, and troubling forces that can disturb a child's emotional tranquillity during the early years of life.

Essentially, this stage in a child's emotional development is normal and very significant. It marks the passing of "infantile" sexuality (which lacks any specific outside target and is felt throughout the body in general) and the beginning of "mature" sexuality (which focuses on a particular love object and is more restricted in feeling to the genitals).

It is assumed that all children go through this stage. However, some are more conscious of their feelings than others, some experience such feelings earlier or later than others, and many offer no easily observable manifestations of such feelings.

Parents of a child who is undergoing this stage of emotional development need to be especially tolerant of any attempts their child makes to bond more closely with a love object and to withdraw from, or compete with, a rival. As distressing or obnoxious as such behaviors can sometimes be, they are early and vital experiments in dealing with adult feelings.

4.
Shyness and Aggression

Every child sometimes behaves shyly and sometimes aggressively. It all depends on the particular social circumstance and the overall emotional state in which that situation is entered. But apart from this dynamic, some children are predisposed to be shy consistently; others are inclined to be aggressive. Most often, their behavior appears to be a matter of inborn temperament.

Recent scientific studies suggest that inherently shy people are more easily aroused physiologically. In other words, their nervous system naturally functions in such a way that they become more quickly and profoundly excited by any change in stimuli. Thus, physicians and mental-health professionals have begun to refer to such people as "highly reactive" rather than "shy."

In highly reactive individuals, the shyness itself is an instinctive behavior designed to protect them from a physiological—and, possibly, emotional—overload. As for inherently aggressive people, science hasn't come up with a similar explanation for why some people are demonstrably more bold, assertive, or uninhibited than the norm.

Apart from a child's intrinsic temperament, there are other explanations for an ongoing tendency to behave either shyly or aggressively. Children under six who are unusually big, small, or ill or who are otherwise very different physically from their surrounding peers might develop either a shy personality to avoid attracting attention or an aggressive personality to compensate for what they perceive as a liability. Family relationships can also play a role. A child raised in a very competitive family may choose either to retreat from the competition by being shy or enter into the competition by being bold.

Birth order is yet another possible factor. For example, the "baby" of a family with numerous children is often inclined to be shy, which may be the net effect of so many other people taking care of her or him. If such a child were compelled to be more independent, a more aggressive personality might emerge. Conversely, the oldest child in a family with numerous children is typically inclined to be bold, perhaps because she or he can claim superiority over the other children or feels responsible for protecting the younger children.

Until a child is around two years old, it's very difficult to identify with any certainty a predisposition toward either shyness or aggression. After the age of two, a child begins to function as a distinctly separate individual and to interact more with others, especially peers. It is during these social encounters that the child's behavior is the most illuminating. If the child tends to let others make decisions, lead in games, do most of the talking, or commandeer all the desired toys, then it's possible that she or he is essentially shy. If the child tends to be the decision maker, the leader, the talker, and the toy grabber, then it's possible that she or he is essentially aggressive.

The degree to which a child likes to touch or hug, or to be touched or hugged, is not a reliable indicator of whether she or he is shy or aggressive by nature. The limits a child sets on body contact with someone else can have many contributing factors, not the least of which may be the relative sensitivity of her or his skin.

For similar reasons, whether a child tends to cling, or not to cling, is also not necessarily an indicator of inherent shyness or aggressiveness. Usually a child outgrows an idiosyncratic need to cling or not to cling by age six. Assuming such behavior isn't accompanied by other disturbing symptoms (for example, consistently crying while refusing to let go of a parent or running away in fear when touched), there's no need to be concerned.

Whatever the case, it's important to realize that shyness and aggression in themselves are neutral attributes—each having its own fair share of positive and negative applications. There is no reason to worry about a child's being basically shy or aggressive unless that personality trait is clearly and repeatedly causing emotional turmoil in the child or in others.

Many parents have difficulty accepting this advice, especially in the case of a shy child. Western culture puts such a premium on aggression in human affairs that parents tend to worry inordinately about their shy child's ability to hold her or his own against others later in life. It's vital for these parents to remind themselves that many creative and successful people have been, and are, shy by nature and that this very trait was a major factor in their success.

On the whole, parents are much less apprehensive about raising an aggressive child. Some parents do worry whether their aggressive child will also turn out to be compassionate; but, again, this is not an issue that requires parental intervention unless definite and irrefutable problems have arisen that are directly attributable to the child's lack of compassion.

Even when an aggressive child does tend to act without a proper degree of compassion, the parents can't expect to change the fundamental predisposition to be aggressive. All they can reasonably hope to do is to change the *manner* in which the child exercises that predisposition. Long-term research indicates that only about one-third of the individuals who are basically shy or basically aggressive as children (combined, an estimated 40 percent of the population) ever change much by the time they are adults.

In the life of a child under six years old, it's unlikely that any major or complicated problems will occur having to do with her or his inherent shyness or aggression (although the likelihood is higher for kids under six who are in day care or nursery schools). Most of the problems for kids under six are situational and easy to spot. Some examples follow:

■ a shy child being regularly bossed around by another child (not necessarily an aggressive one);

■ an aggressive child regularly making other children cry (not necessarily shy ones);

■ a shy child refusing to come out of her or his room when company visits and wants to see her or him;

■ an aggressive child disturbing everyone at a family gathering by demanding constant attention.

After a child reaches age six, at which time academic and social pressures increase enormously, her or his natural shyness or aggression can become much more problematic. Therefore, it is wise to be on the lookout for a consistent pattern of shyness or aggression in the behavior of your child *under* six so that you can intervene at critical moments by giving your shy child a gentle push or by gently restraining your aggressive child. Just be sure to proceed with caution. A few incidents do not a shy or a bold child make. And the majority of children do not seem to have a strong predisposition in either direction.

Managing a Child's Shyness

Here are guidelines for helping your child deal with problems she or he may be having, or creating, as a result of being inherently shy:

■ *Focus your attention on each situation as it happens, not on your child's personality or overall behavior.*

Your six-year-old is too young to understand generalities. If you accuse her or him of being too shy or refer to any history of inappropriately shy behavior, you will simply confuse your child, creating even more feelings of helplessness and hopelessness.

Only address the issue of shyness as it relates to an incident that is very fresh in your child's memory. Structure your remarks so that they refer to the problematic nature of the situation itself, not the "wrongness" of the way your child acted. For example, if your child has a miserable time at a party because she or he is too shy to enter into the party games, lead her or him to see how the games—or the people playing them—might appear scary in some way but in fact are nonthreatening and even fun. You might even try playing the very same games with your child at appropriate times so that she or he can come to enjoy them better.

■ *Make sure your child knows that she or he has a right to express feelings and needs.*

After an episode of shyness, elicit from your child what her or his feelings and needs were at the time. Indicate that it is all right not only to have such feelings and needs but also to act on them in relationships with others.

If your child is not forthcoming on these issues, try simply telling your child about her or his rights in such matters either by referring directly to the incident at hand or by sharing a story that refers to the incident indirectly. You might also help your child release repressed emotions by suggesting that she or he draw a picture or play a particular game.

■ *Engage your child in activities that will help bolster self-confidence.*

First, identify those activities that your child seems to enjoy and master. Then praise your child for skill in those activities and encourage more frequent participation in them.

To deal with specific situations in which your child appears to lack self-confidence, some form of role-playing or "rehearsal" might be helpful. Ask your child to join you in creating an imaginary version of the target situation—one in which the child can feel safer and more empowered. Shy children often see their own way out of their shyness once they are asked to put themselves in a bolder child's shoes or pretend that they are doing something they've been too shy to do in real life.

■ *When possible, help ease your child into potentially difficult situations.*

If you realize ahead of time that your child is likely to be shy about interacting with another person or taking part in a certain event, be sure to do what you can to smooth the path. Don't be obviously directorial; work subtly to do whatever you can to make the difficult situation less threatening.

Before it occurs, let your child know what to expect and encourage a positive attitude. Just take care not to be too dramatic in your description of the event. Otherwise, your child might feel pressured to have a similar response to it.

Arrange your child's actual entrance into the event so that it occurs at a good time for the child and isn't too abrupt or overwhelming. As much as you can without coddling, assist the child in becoming acclimated to the situation before leaving her or him alone.

■ *Tactfully intervene in situations where you witness another child taking unfair advantage of your child.*

When your shy child is playing with another child or with other children, it's not appropriate for you to watch over them like a hawk. You may only reinforce your child's tendency to lack self-reliance. However, it is appropriate to check into the play situation very discreetly from time to time.

If you happen to see your child being treated unfairly during one of your "check-ins," step into the situation and clarify calmly and simply who has what rights. At any age, but especially when they are under six years old, children need adult help in such matters. They are not always able—or willing— to sort them out on their own.

■ *Praise your child's efforts at being more independent and more constructively assertive.*

Whenever your child does behave in a manner that is self-confident and appropriately bold, be sure to point out how much you admire that act. Again, the focus should be on what the child *did*, not on the *child*.

■ *Set a good example of self-confidence and self-assertion.*
Children in general notice far more than their parents think they do; this may be especially true in the case of shy children, who tend to be very reflective. Let your child see you standing up for your rights when it's necessary or taking the initiative in a difficult or novel situation.

Managing an Aggressive Child

Here are guidelines for assisting your child in dealing with problems she or he may be having, or creating, as a result of being inherently aggressive:

■ *Make it clear that you disapprove of what happened in a specific situation and not of your child.*
Aggressive children are quick to become angry or resentful, especially if they feel their very identity is being attacked. Accept your child for who she or he is and direct your remarks about aggression toward each negative situation as it comes to your attention.

■ *Teach your child to appreciate that other people have rights and needs that must be respected.*
Referring to a very recent situation in which your child ignored or violated someone else's rights, you should establish what those rights were and why they needed to be respected. Aside from direct discussion, one of the best ways to do this is to role-play, giving your child the other person's part.

In your role-play, re-create the specific situation in which your child behaved with inappropriate aggression and then handle that situation more appropriately. For example, suppose that your child recently caused a problem by grabbing a playmate's toy. In your role-play of this situation, you as your child should politely ask for permission to play with the toy. If that permission is not granted, then you should bargain politely to see if you can work out a compromise (e.g., playing with the toy in a couple of minutes). If that doesn't work, then you should accept the other child's judgment and find something of your own with which to play.

A subtler way to teach appreciation for others' rights is by telling rights-related stories and then engaging your child in a discussion of them. You might also try exposing your child to television programs or movies that you know discuss rights in a manner that is appropriate to your child's age level and rights-related experiences.

■ Engage your child in activities that will exercise her or his capacities for self-control and compassion.
Whenever someone close is in need of help or attention, propose to your child something that she or he might do: make a card, a visit, a phone call or do some simple task for the other person's benefit. Some aggressive children are "tamed" by learning to care for a pet.

■ Anticipate problematic situations and let your child know what you expect.
Faced with a situation in which you know your child may be inappropriately assertive, take a few moments to discuss how you'd like to see things go. Avoid being accusatory. Simply enlist your child's natural "take-charge" proclivity in making the event a pleasant one for every person involved. Aggressive children have an unfortunate tendency to act before they think, and this kind of preparatory strategy session helps circumvent that tendency.

■ If you actually see your child abusing another child's rights, don't hesitate to referee.
Self-management is a very troublesome task for an aggressive child, so your calm intervention in a deteriorating situation can keep matters from getting totally out of hand. Guard against being punitive. Clarify what's fair given the situation at hand, gain everyone's commitment to fair play, and then withdraw.

■ Always praise appropriate self-control.
When your normally aggressive child deliberately exercises self-discipline due to a sense of compassion or fairness, let her or him know at the soonest appropriate moment that you're very proud of that behavior.

■ Set a good example of fairness and self-control.

The more your child sees you acknowledging the rights of others, the more she or he will be prepared to do the same. What doesn't come naturally to a child needs to be role modeled.

Caught in the Act

Taylor and Mike, both age four, had been good playmates for almost a year. One day, when Mike showed Taylor his new toy truck, Taylor yelled, "Give that to me!" and grabbed for it. Mike let him take it out of his hands and immediately started crying.

Taylor's father, who had observed the scene, knelt down next to Taylor and said in a soft voice, "I know how much you'd like to play with that truck, but it's not yours. It's Mike's. And he feels bad now that you've taken it away from him. Please give it back to him now. Later on, you can ask him in a nice way if you could play with it for just a little while. Okay?" Taylor agreed and returned the truck. In a few moments, the friends resumed playing together happily.

Mike's mother had also observed the scene. She did nothing at the time because Taylor's father stepped in to handle matters. Afterward, however, she recalled the scene for Mike and asked him, "Why didn't you say no to Taylor and keep him from grabbing your truck?" Mike, clearly confused by his own behavior, could only answer, "Taylor's my friend."

Wanting to help Mike realize that he would not have lost Taylor's friendship just by refusing to give him the truck, Mike's mother asked her son to pretend that Taylor had a new toy car. "Would you stop being Taylor's friend if he didn't let you play with his car one time?" she asked. "No," Mike answered with conviction. Sometimes children need a little parental coaching to see their way out of misconceptions.

5.
Fear

Children under the age of six live in a world that is far more baffling and emotionally challenging than their parents can comprehend, despite having been children once themselves. In this "under six" world, everything remains relatively new and therefore potentially unsettling.

To complicate matters, it's difficult for the very young inhabitants of this world to distinguish between what is real (like the death of a grandparent) and what is imaginary (like the death of a similar person on television or in a dream). Each passing hour can bring a fresh round of puzzlement, surprise, and shock; and as children under six live through these hours, they are acutely aware of their smallness and powerlessness compared to adults.

Although parents may not be able to reenter the confusing world of the very young, they can certainly appreciate that children living in such a world are bound to experience a wide range of different kinds, as well as many individual incidents, of fear. The true wonder of childhood is that children are usually able to grow through their fears so quickly—a powerful testament to their inner resources of hope, rationality, and self-preservation.

When parents are faced with their children's fears, the biggest single problem besetting them is an agonizing tendency toward over-protectiveness. You can't possibly shield your child from all fears; and even if you could, it wouldn't always be wise to do so. Giving vent to fear can often be an effective and healthy way for a child to deal with a troubling situation. For example, a fear of dogs can inspire a child to develop safer, more respectful, and more rewarding conduct toward animals of all kinds. A fear of separation from a parent teaches a child to appreciate caretaking, manage anger, and feel empathy for people in need of human contact.

What you as a parent can and should do is to monitor your child's fears in a discreet and practical manner so that you can help your child process more significant fears as constructively as possible. If a certain fear is not seriously disabling and doesn't last longer than three or four weeks at a stretch, there's no need to worry about your child's overall emotional health. However, if a certain fear continues to preoccupy your child for more than a month or if it prevents your child from leading a normal life, then therapy should be considered. It's also wise to check with a professional whenever an episode of strong fear triggers physical symptoms in your child, such as a rapid heartbeat, dizziness, headache, nausea, or incontinence.

Timely and intelligent handling of unusually strong childhood fears is essential for both the present and the future emotional health of a child under six. Left to itself, a persistent or especially severe childhood fear can ultimately lead to an adult phobia: an ongoing, intractable, and unreasonable anxiety regarding something in particular. Among the more common phobias of this type are acrophobia (fear of heights), claustrophobia (fear of enclosed spaces), and any one of a number of animal-related phobias (like entomophobia, or fear of insects).

Until your child is able to communicate fears verbally, there is little you can do except to "read" them through your child's nonverbal behavior and then minimize the grounds for them as much as practically possible. Once your child is capable of conversing with you about these fears, there are a number of ways that you can help her or him manage them so that they don't turn into serious problems:

1. Respond to your child's fear with equanimity and compassion.
Be respectful of your child's feelings but not overly solicitous. A shower of concern and attention not only rewards a child for being afraid but also risks scaring her or him into being even more fearful.

Conversely, don't belittle or dismiss the fear or resort to teasing or anger in an effort to change the fearful attitude. If your child sees these types of responses, she or he may cease to complain of fear, but chances are strong that the fear will still be present, all the more emotionally injurious for being suppressed.

2. Gently encourage your child to discuss the fear.
Being careful not to express your own opinions prematurely, ask your child to describe her or his fearful experience(s) and feeling(s). The more informed you are about the nature of the fear, the better you can help your child deal with it. At the same time, the more your child talks about the fear, the more likely she or he is to work through it.

Don't press if your child is reluctant to discuss the fear in much detail. Otherwise, you may unwittingly force her or him to become frightened all over again. If your child says that she or he doesn't want to talk about it, comment that you are really interested in knowing more about it, giving her or him a second chance to talk. If your child insists on remaining silent, leave it at that.

Whether or not your child is willing to talk about the fear, you might try inviting her or him to express the fear in a drawing. Children are often much more comfortable creating visual images than they are expressing themselves verbally, and the results can be even more therapeutic.

3. Reassure your child regarding the feared object or situation and her or his own coping skills.

Be honest in your assessments. If possible, speak from your personal experience of encountering similar objects or situations and of observing your child's displays of courage and resourcefulness in analogous circumstances.

4. Engage your child in discussing constructive ways to cope with the fear.

Coax your child to volunteer ideas before offering your personal suggestions. A child will be much more interested in carrying through a plan that she or he has personally generated. At the end of such a discussion, work toward some form of commitment, no matter how tentative, to a particular plan. Be careful not to make the plan too detailed or time-specific so that there's no serious risk of failure.

5. Be especially patient with your child.

As much as possible, allow your child to confront and master the fear at her or his own pace. For a brief time after the fear develops, your child may need to go through a passive period of self-recovery without taking any direct action to overcome the fear. Give your child up to several weeks before expecting to see any improvement.

If necessary, you can gently move things along by engineering situations in which your child can *gradually* come to terms with the fear. This step-by-step acclimatization technique is used to cure adult phobias. Suppose, for example, that your child is afraid of dogs, is apparently unable to overcome this fear on her or his own initiative, and is routinely exposed to dogs at the homes of playmates and relatives. First, you might arrange a special time for you and your child to observe puppies from a safe distance, such as at a pet store. If that experience is pleasurable, you might then set up a secure situation in which your child can pet a puppy for as long a time, or as short a time, as she or he wishes. If all goes well, you might take the next step: giving your child an opportunity to spend some supervised time with a full-grown dog—during which time you can teach your child specific coping skills.

6. *Encourage your child to engage in activities that will serve to counterbalance the fear.*

Physical play helps many people discharge feelings of hostility, frustration, or depression—all feelings that can underlie, or accompany, a specific case of fearfulness. Drawing and performing small tasks can serve the same purpose, plus these activities enable children to prove to themselves that they *can* exercise self-control and mastery over the outside world.

7. *Tactfully watch and support your child's progress in coping with fear.*

Without repeatedly compelling your child to report her or his fear-related experiences and feelings to you, keep track of how she or he appears to be managing the fear. If you witness your child confronting a formerly feared object or situation in a competent, self-assured manner or if your child tells you about such a confrontation, be sure to offer your praise.

8. *Set a good example.*

In developing a fear of something, your child may be taking cues from you. Watch what you say and do to make sure you aren't inadvertently and inappropriately communicating anxiety to your child.

9. *Anticipate potentially fearful situations and take reasonable measures to make them less fearful.*

You don't want to be overprotective with your child, but this doesn't mean you can't be protective to an appropriate degree. For example, if you know your child has a fear of strangers and you're about to hire a new baby-sitter, make arrangements for your child to spend some time with the sitter in advance, while you are present. If your child fears scary-looking faces, it may be a good idea not to have her or him waiting at the door when Halloween trick-or-treaters come by or to ask the latter to let your child see their real faces underneath their masks.

A Timetable for Fears

Children typically experience different types of fears at different stages in their physical, cognitive, and emotional development. Among the most prevalent age-appropriate fears are the following:

BIRTH TO SIX MONTHS

- any loud and sudden noise
- any quick movement on the part of another person
- falling or being dropped
- loss of support in general

SEVEN MONTHS TO ONE YEAR

- specific loud noises (such as a garbage disposal)
- strangers in general
- being dressed, undressed, or changed
- tub and basin drains (where the child bathes)
- heights
- helplessness when faced with unexpected situations

ONE TO TWO YEARS

- specific loud noises
- separation from a parent
- strangers in general
- tub and basin drains (where the child bathes)
- sleeping in general (loss of consciousness and nightmares)
- personal injury
- loss of control over physical and emotional functions

TWO TO TWO AND A HALF YEARS

- specific loud noises
- separation from, or rejection by, a parent
- strange peers
- toilets (especially flushing)
- nightmares
- changes in the environment (e.g., moved furniture, altered living spaces)
- bad weather (especially thunder and lightning)

TWO AND A HALF TO THREE YEARS

■ large, looming objects

■ strange peers

■ unusual occurrences and changes in routine

■ loss or movement of objects

■ nightmares

CASE:

Weathering the Storm

When Carly was two and a half years old, she developed a fear of storms. She would get quiet and watchful whenever the sky turned dark. If it began to rain heavily, she would start crying. Thunder and lightning would elicit shrieks of terror.

Carly's parents decided to distract her attention from storms by turning stormy times into party times. When a storm hit, they would announce, "Time for a party!" Then they would lay out a blanket in the family room, play with some of Carly's toys, listen to music, and eat special treats.

The first three times Carly's parents did this, she would forget her fear for short intervals while the party was going on, but a rise in the wind or a sharp peal of thunder frequently prompted another spell of anxious behavior. By the fourth storm party, however, she was no longer surprised by feelings of fear, and she continued to remain composed after the party, even though the storm was still raging.

Eventually, a full-fledged, parent-run storm party was no longer necessary. Carly had learned to seek entertaining distraction on her own.

CASE:

Battle of the Bugs

One afternoon four-year-old Jason was helping his father clean the garage. He balked when it came to removing some empty boxes from a dark corner, telling his father, "I don't want any bugs to get me."

The first thing Jason's father did was to try to put this fear into perspective. "What *kind* of bugs?" he asked. "Flying bugs," Jason answered. Later, they consulted a book of insects, and Jason's father asked him to indicate which "flying bugs" were the worst and which weren't really so bad. This activity made both Jason and his father realize that what scared him the most were flying insects that made noises: droning houseflies and beetles and buzzing bees, hornets, wasps, and mosquitoes.

With the assistance of the insect book and a rented videotape, Jason's father helped him appreciate the lives that these insects led and the roles that they played in the biological scheme of things: providing food, transferring pollen, decomposing waste matter, and fertilizing the soil. He also managed to trap individual specimens of some of the feared insects under a drinking glass so that Jason could observe them safely at a close distance. Armed with this new understanding of his former enemies, Jason lost his fear within a couple of weeks.

Managing Fear of the Hospital

When your very young child needs to stay in the hospital overnight or longer for medical tests, treatment, or surgery, don't assume that she or he will be afraid of the experience in the same way that an adult would be. Most very young children harbor no preconceptions of what a hospital visit, a serious illness, medical care, or a painful recuperation might entail. If your child does exhibit fear (and some do not), it's almost certainly because of this lack of knowledge as well as the fact that she or he is leaving home, loved ones, and familiar daily routines.

Here are some suggestions for preventing or handling a very young child's fear of the hospital:

■ Seek advice from your physician.

Your physician has no doubt dealt with such fear many times and knows techniques and resources that may help you. Furthermore, she or he can alert you to potential fear-provoking aspects related to the specific situation at hand. In any event, your physician will be able to put your child's fear into perspective for everyone's peace of mind.

■ *Fully inform your child, in a manner appropriate to her or his intelligence level, about what is going to happen.*

Don't lie to your child or make promises that may not come true (e.g., "It won't hurt," "You'll enjoy it," or "I'll be with you all the time"). As soon as you're able, go over the realities of the situation without instilling undue anxiety but also without leaving your child unprepared for the possible pain or fear that may be involved.

■ *If practical, let your child visit the hospital in advance and witness you talking with the physician about the visit.*

This will eliminate a great deal of the shock element when it's time for your child's scheduled stay. Your physician, or someone on the hospital staff, can probably help arrange this exploratory visit so that your child has a pleasant time.

■ *Plan something fun for your child to do after the hospital stay.*

Anticipation of this posthospital event will help your child put up with some of the negative things that may occur while in the hospital.

■ *Accompany your child as much as practical or possible during the hospital stay.*

Some hospitals have facilities for a parent to stay overnight or longer with the child. Many allow a parent to accompany the child into operating and treatment rooms. Whatever the situation, let your child know when to expect your presence during the hospital stay and when not to (reassuring your child, in the latter case, that you will be waiting for her or him afterward).

■ *When the hospital experience is over, continue to refer to it casually as long as it still seems to be on the child's mind.*

This strategy invites your child to share—and thereby discharge—any residual fears or confusions about the experience.

At PCGC:
Pain Management for
Very Young Children

Compared to all that we know about the emotional and physiological factors relating to *adult* pain, there is a surprising lack of information and education about the emotional and physiological factors relating to *children*'s pain. As a result, many misconceptions exist, such as the false notions that children, especially infants, do not feel pain as intensely as adults and that they are essentially incapable of managing the pain they do feel.

The best way for hospitals and clinics to assist child patients and their families in coping more intelligently with severe or chronic pain is to coordinate medical, psychological, nursing, physical therapy, and technological resources into an integrated treatment plan. Increasingly, hospitals and clinics are aiming in this direction.

The guiding philosophy of this kind of "pain management" plan is to minimize the child's pain as much as possible while at the same time increasing her or his ability to function. For example, in the Pain Management Program conducted by The Children's Hospital of Philadelphia and the Philadelphia Child Guidance Center, a pain management team of professionals is assigned to each case. To treat the physical aspects of pain, physicians on these teams rely on new medications, old medications used in new ways, and innovative techniques in administering medications. To address the psychological aspects of pain, psychiatrists and psychologists on these teams rely on various nonmedical methods to help the child cope with pain and to assist the family in managing stress factors associated with the pain. Among these nonmedical methods are the following:

ACTIVE LISTENING

Children in pain often feel that other people—especially adults—are incapable of understanding or appreciating what they are going through. Team members always exercise active listening skills when they are working with a child, and they teach family members and caretakers to do the same. Here are the main active listening skills:

■ establishing trust with the child;

■ encouraging the child to talk openly about painful experiences;

■ not interrupting or "speaking for" the child;

■ never questioning what the child says about her or his pain;

■ demonstrating that you understand and respect what the child has said.

BIOFEEDBACK

Using a computer, child patients are able to see or hear their own physiological reaction to pain. This helps them put the pain into a more realistic perspective and inspires them to work effectively toward reducing it.

For example, a girl with chronic leg pain can attach computer-connected electrodes to her leg and then engage in very simple relaxation techniques aimed at easing her leg pain. As these techniques change the level of her skin conductivity, thus indicating a relaxation of her leg pain, she sees the change registered by the computer: A train appears on the screen and runs downhill on a track. Through this kind of activity, she learns to channel her attentive energies more and more toward *controlling* her physiological reaction instead of just *expressing* her discomfort.

SELF-HYPNOSIS AND RELAXATION

Many techniques exist for teaching a child how to relax, including deep muscle relaxation or visual imagery. The techniques chosen for a specific case depend on the age of the patient and the nature of the pain.

Take, for instance, the relatively extreme case of a five-year-old boy with cancer who is frightened of bone-marrow aspirations. His anxiety makes the procedure even more painful than it naturally is. To alleviate this anxiety, the boy can be taught to visualize an imaginary line running from the back of his neck to the place on his body where he feels that pain and then to imagine that he himself is turning the wire on and off. Eventually, he can learn to "let go" of his pain when the wire is "off" and thereby tolerate the temporary procedure with much less discomfort.

PAIN DIARY

A pain diary is a written account—often supplemented with simple drawings, charts, or graphs—of when and where the pain occurs, what seems to precipitate the pain, and how intense the pain is (e.g., on a "pain is . . ." scale of "slight," "bad," "very bad," or "awful"). By assisting a child in keeping such an account, family members can help themselves and their child gain a more tangible understanding of the pain and therefore have more control over pain-related experiences.

FAMILY COUNSELING

Counseling for some or all of the child's family members can help ease ongoing or intermittent tensions that may be contributing to the child's pain. In addition, such counseling can teach family members how to cope with the personal and interpersonal difficulties caused specifically by the child's illness as well as how to assist the child in coping more effectively with her or his pain, given the overall family situation at hand.

Look for hospitals or clinics in your area that provide pain management programs similar to the program described above. If none is available, consult your physician or mental-health professional about creating a similar kind of treatment plan for your child.

6.

Depression and

Stress

A human being is never too young to be depressed or stressed out. However, the nature of potential depression and stress varies according to age. For children under six, such experiences are, thank goodness, relatively overt and fleeting. Annoying as it may be for a parent to endure several hours of intermittent crying and whining, it's better on the whole for both parties than if the child were to respond to the same depressing or stressful stimulus with several uninterrupted days of secret suffering.

This doesn't mean that depression or stress is not as important an issue for a very young child as it is for an older child or adult. If ignored or handled inappropriately, it can create an emotional vulnerability in a very young child that may last throughout life, rendering future episodes of depression or stress all the more difficult to prevent, endure, or combat.

Technically, depression refers to a state of sadness characterized by emotional despair and physical lethargy. In very young children, depression can sometimes manifest itself in a disguised form, for example, as anger, irritability, or hyperactivity; but this kind of "disguised" depression (i.e., depression revealing itself in nonstereotypical ways) is far more common among older children and adults.

Almost always, no matter how old the victim, depression is triggered by a loss or sense of loss. In the case of a person this young, it's usually associated with major changes affecting the family at large, such as those attending severe marital discord or separation, a divorce, a remarriage, a sudden health crisis, a death, or a family move.

In contrast to a depressive episode, a stress reaction is a very generalized "shock" response to any event that is especially unfamiliar and disturbing, such as experiencing a period of unusual activity at home, witnessing a violent crime on television, or hearing about a major car accident that occurred down the street. The stress response typically manifests itself as some combination of two or more of the following emotions: fear, disgust, resentment, hate, anger, panic, or overexcitement.

To a child under six, so much of life is disturbing and/or unfamiliar that one might expect frequent stress reactions of high intensity. In fact, children in this age range are inclined to be so emotionally resilient that stress reactions of any significance—ones that last longer than a couple of hours for two- to three-year-olds and longer than a couple of days for four- to six-year-olds—are fairly few and far between.

Because depression and stress in a very young child are so likely to accompany each other or result in similar emotional manifestations, they can be managed in the same basic manner:

■ *Always take seriously any indication that your child is depressed or having a stress reaction.*

Emotionally speaking, a child is weakest at such times. You can easily make matters worse by insisting that her or his feelings are inappropriate, making light of them, or ignoring them altogether.

While you don't want to respond to a depressive episode or a stress reaction with visible anxiety, take care to deal directly and compassionately with *every* such episode that comes to your attention. The potential cost of not doing so to the future emotional health of your child can be great—certainly too great to risk.

■ *Work gently to clarify the cause of the depression or stress reaction and why it is manifesting itself the way it is.*

Without pressuring your child to respond, ask questions that will tell you more specifically *what happened* to make her or him depressed or stressed out and *how she or he feels* about that situation or event. Try to avoid such leading questions as "Was it [x] that made you so scared?" You may inadvertently put words in your child's mouth or give your child yet another reason to be upset. Of course, if this strategy doesn't work and the situation is relatively serious, then it may be advisable to ask your child if she or he is concerned about particular things that you feel may be involved.

It's also a good idea to talk with other knowledgeable people inside or outside the family about the possible cause and effect of your child's depression or stress reaction. Just be careful to give your child's testimony the most weight. Also, make sure that your child's self-esteem and relationships with others won't be negatively influenced by your investigation. For example, don't let your child overhear you discussing her or him with someone else; and don't reveal anything to your other children that might embarrass her or him unless you think it's absolutely necessary.

■ *Allow your child to express emotions freely, without interruption or censorship.*

At first, be patient with outbursts that are unkind, misinformed, irrational, or otherwise objectionable. Then, after the child has reached a stopping point, make your own contribution toward putting your child in a better frame of mind.

This strategy not only provides you with more insight into your child's problem; it also provides your child with an opportunity to release negative feelings and, in the process, discover more positive ones.

■ *Offer consoling information and support.*

Make sure your child is not suffering from gross misconceptions about what has occurred, what is going to occur, or the extent to which these occurrences are threatening. Without lying, reassure your child that she or he is loved and is safe. Offer to do whatever you can to make her or him feel better.

It's fine to propose remedies or distractions to your child but don't indicate that she or he is wrong not to accept one of them. A vital part of the support you need to offer in such a situation is letting your child know—directly or indirectly—that you are willing to allow her or him to go through this period at her or his own pace.

■ *Do what you can behind the scenes to alleviate your child's depression or stress reaction.*

Try to maintain a home atmosphere that is peaceful. Minimize the chances that your child will be exposed to emotionally jarring situations in real life, on television, or in the movies. Give your child the freedom to do as she or he wishes, within reason; but also be prepared to give your child a reasonable amount of extra attention if it is sought.

■ *Observe closely how you, your child, and other family members handle your child's depression or stress reaction for as long as it lasts.*

How an incident of depression is handled can reveal a great deal about each member of the household, and family dynamics in general, that you might not otherwise notice. Over time, you may discern a pattern in how you, your child, and other members of the family instigate, manage, or fail to manage your child's periods of depression or stress reactions. If you should ever have to seek professional help to cope with your child's intractable, recurring, or unusually severe depression or stress reaction, such background information can be extremely valuable.

■ *Anticipate the occurrence of similar incidents of depression or stress reaction in the future.*

Armed with the knowledge you've gained from specific incidents of depression or stress reaction in the past, you can take steps to prevent or forestall future incidents of a like nature or prepare your child and other family members to manage them more effectively.

For example, if you know from experience that your child gets upset when not permitted to go on special trips with older siblings, you might do the following:

■ In a casual, conversational manner, inform your child ahead of time about the special excursion so that she or he doesn't feel left out of a secret.

■ Make sure that your older children know about this delicate situation and that they take care not to brag about the trip in their younger sibling's presence.

■ Set up in advance something special that your child can look foward to doing at the same time as the excursion.

■ Arrange for your child to be away at the precise time that older siblings leave home.

Coping with a Divorce

Very young children can understand two friends or two siblings having a quarrel and separating for a certain amount of time thereafter, but their minds can't process all the ramifications of a divorce. They tend to confuse a divorce with a death: Whatever it may be, it means that someone (in this case, Mommy or Daddy—or both, in cases of split custody) won't be around as much anymore. Mercifully, their short-term emotional reaction to either a death or a divorce is apt to be fairly subdued as long as the event isn't accompanied by violent outbursts or radical changes in the child's day-to-day life.

To date, there is no reliable research establishing whether it is better for children of *any* age if their divorced parents continue to live together, split custodial responsibilities, or assign such responsibilities to only one of the parents. Nor has one particular type of visitation pattern proven to be the most successful (assuming the pattern itself is regular and dependable). Too much depends on the individuals involved: The specific divorce arrangement that works for one family may not work at all for another.

However, if you and your spouse are divorcing, there are some generally effective guidelines you can follow to help your very young child accept and endure the divorce with a minimal amount of emotional turmoil:

■ *As soon as possible, let your child know that you are divorcing but that she or he will continue to receive the love and care of both parents.*

Preferably, you and your spouse will make this announcement together, sending a signal to your child that both you and your spouse are in agreement about the divorce and that all of you will be sharing the experience. Check to make sure that your child realizes not only that you are not going to stay married or live together anymore but also that each of you will continue to be active participants in your child's life.

■ *Assure your child that she or he is not in any way responsible for the divorce.*

Children are very self-centered by nature. Never underestimate their capacity to feel that the divorce is somehow their fault or that their love for both parents should be enough to make their parents abandon the idea of divorcing. Take every appropriate opportunity to remind your child that the divorce is the result of irrevocable differences between mother and father and is not due to anything that concerns her or him.

■ *As the divorce unfolds, keep your child informed.*

Often the most difficult part of a divorce for a very young child is being aware that something "big" is going on but not actually knowing what's happening. Left in complete ignorance, the child is free to imagine that things are worse than they really are or to hope for the best—only to be cruelly disappointed later on.

It isn't appropriate to share with your child *all* the stress-producing details and feelings associated with ironing out your divorce arrangements, but your child should be kept up to date in general terms on such matters as:

■ When is the noncustodial parent leaving?

■ Where will the noncustodial parent be living?

■ When can your child next expect to see the noncustodial parent?

■ How frequently—and in what context(s)—will she or he be able to see the noncustodial parent in the future?

■ When can she or he next expect to see both parents at the same time?

■ How frequently—and in what context(s)—will she or he be able to see both parents together in the future?

■ When will the divorce be official?

■ What happens after the divorce is official?

No matter how specific you can or cannot be in answering these questions, the ongoing dialogue concerning these matters will afford your child the opportunity to come to terms with the change that is largely taking place behind her or his back.

■ *Try not to disrupt the normal pattern and tenor of your child's day-to-day life.*

The more familiar the rest of your child's daily life is, the more secure she or he will be in the face of any changes caused by the divorce. Don't impose "new order" rules and routines at home unless they are absolutely necessary because of the absence of the other parent. You need to allow your child to appreciate that a parental divorce does not mean the end of the world.

■ *Guard against taking out your frustrations over the divorce on your child.*

Although it may be very difficult, try not to alter your behavior toward your child during the divorce. Don't lean on her or him more heavily for emotional support, don't become more critical of her or his conduct or attributes, and don't demand that she or he be more understanding because of what you are going through.

■ *Maintain good communication and cooperation between yourself and the other parent regarding matters affecting the child.*

Don't allow your child to see or hear the two of you fighting about her or him and don't slip in your responsibility to keep the other parent informed about the child you share. If you and the other parent are able to demonstrate to your child that you are equally well informed about her or his life and that you are acting in concert regarding her or his welfare, your child will adjust to the divorce much more smoothly and readily.

Coping with a Remarriage

Assuming a child under six has gradually become familiar with a parent's spouse-to-be before the actual wedding, the remarriage should be accepted with very few problems, if any. A child this young is not nearly as inclined as an older child to compete with the new stepparent for her or his natural parent's affection or to resent the new stepparent's assumption of a role that once belonged to her or his other natural parent.

To ensure that your remarriage gets off to a good start without serious emotional repercussions to your child under six, follow these steps:

■ *Make sure that you and your partner agree on how to raise your child.*

This will prevent arguments between the two of you about the child that could wind up making her or him feel insecure. Ideally, your child should continue to be raised in the manner that's familiar, at least for a while. Any changes should be introduced very gradually.

■ *Talk privately with your child about your new partner and the marriage.*

You and your new partner should make an effort to do many things *together* with your child so that your child will accept the two of you as a parental team. Just remember that it is also important for you to spend some time *alone* with your child during which you can discuss her or his new stepparent and this new phase of family life.

Don't pressure your child to reveal her or his feelings. They may not be very strong or identifiable, given her or his young age and lack of experience with such matters. Instead, reveal your own feelings first and then ask if your child has any questions or thoughts about what's happening.

This is your opportunity to clear up any misconceptions your child may have about your partner as an individual, the role of a stepparent in general (often misconstrued as a threatening one because of fairy tales), the role and feelings of the other natural parent, and/or the remarriage. Even if your child has no questions or misconceptions, she or he will appreciate the fact that you are concerned and that you value her or his opinion.

■ *Frequently reassure your child of your continuing love and devotion.*

As you spend more and more time with your partner, your child needs to hear more and more often that you care just as much about her or him and will always be there to provide comfort and safety.

■ *As much as practical, indulge any tendencies your child may have to cling to you or to your new partner.*

It is normal for children during this period to cling to their natural parent, because they fear losing a love they've had all their life, or to the new partner, because they're afraid she or he will "go away," as the former partner did. In either case, don't be too quick to discourage the clinging as long as it isn't interfering with your plans. Your child can benefit from a heightened sense of security and some extra affection at this time.

■ *Don't be concerned if your child doesn't respond as enthusiastically to the marriage as you had hoped.*

Your child may seem emotionally "flat" during the transition period. If so, she or he is probably just waiting to see what happens. Again, children under six have a very limited concept of what a marriage or a remarriage means, so they can't be expected to rise to the occasion automatically.

■ *Be sure to allow times for you and your partner to enjoy your relationship apart from your child.*

Often new couples make the mistake of catering to their very young child so much that they deny themselves the time alone together that they need to maintain a strong and loving relationship. In the long run, this time alone together is also essential to the child's well-being, since it tends to make the couple more effective in their parenting and to teach the child to be more independent.

Make an effort to spend some time alone with your partner each day. Above all, avoid taking your child on your honeymoon. If it is completely impractical to leave the child with someone else right after the wedding, then postpone the honeymoon until it *is* practical.

Coping with Bad News

Very young children do not react to traumatic and stressful events in the same way that older children or adults do. When they hear about, or witness, something scary happening, they lack the cognitive ability to judge such an event in terms of why it happened, what it means, and whether it threatens them directly. Instead, their reaction is entirely emotional and can easily escalate into full-fledged panic or depression. Here are some tips for preventing such an emotional overreaction.

■ *Control your child's exposure to potentially disturbing images on television, in movies, and in printed materials.*
The line between fantasy and reality is very faint and flexible to a child under six. A make-believe image is just as likely to be frightening as a true-life happening.

As much as practically possible, don't allow your child to see shows or materials that may contain upsetting subject matter. If you're not sure whether a specific program your child wants to watch will be upsetting, watch it with your child so that you can offer reassurance and explanation at appropriate moments (e.g., a comment that the actors are just pretending, a description of how a particularly disturbing special effect might have been achieved, or a guarantee that what is happening on-screen won't happen to your child).

■ *Talk with your child as soon as possible about upsetting incidents in real life that are likely to reach her or his attention.*
This includes family crises (e.g., a serious illness, a marital separation, or a job loss), calamities in the neighborhood (a murder or a building burning down), and major national and international catastrophes (a war or an earthquake). You don't need to say much. Indeed, saying too much may frighten your child. And children at this stage in their development can't fully comprehend such matters as death, the economic problems attending a reversal in family fortune, or the reason why one group of people are fighting with another.

Whatever the crisis, calamity, or catastrophe, the best course of action is simply to inform your child about it in a simple, nondramatic way and to reaffirm your child's personal safety and security. Hearing about the event first from you rather than some other source will make it seem less alarming. In addition, your taking the initiative in this way leaves the door open for the child to communicate to you—then or later— any particular fears he or she may experience related to the event.

■ *Be alert for signs that your child is responding over-anxiously to bad news.*
Common signs that a child is experiencing stress include nightmares, aggressive play, long periods of withdrawal or silence, increased attachment to one or both parents, loss of appetite, or an increase in angry or irritable behavior. You shouldn't worry about these responses unless they become excessive, at which point you should talk with the child about her or his stressful feelings and do what you can to alleviate them by offering reassurance and distraction.

■ *Help your child discharge anxiety in constructive ways.*
Many children respond well to drawing or role-playing about what is bothering them or to hearing stories that offer soothing commentary relative to the disturbing event. Depending on the situation, your child may actually be able to take a positive role in the event: for example, by making a get-well card for a sick person.

Coping with a Death

Until children reach the age of five or six, they can't begin to understand what death really means. The most prevalent misconception is that death, like sleep, is a temporary state of being that can be reversed. Television cartoons, fairy tales, and "play dead" games feed this misconception, as does the inexplicable (to them) appearance and disappearance of people in their day-to-day lives.

Lacking the ability to appreciate the permanence and gravity of death, very young children are not likely to respond to a specific death with strong emotions. An exception may be if a child actually witnesses a sudden and shocking death, such as a parent suffering a massive heart attack or a pet being run over by a car. In such a case, the child will no doubt have a much more severe stress reaction than in cases where the death is not witnessed or is less violent.

Whatever the case, a child this young does not appear to experience the type of immediate, prolonged, and demonstrative grieving period for a dead loved one that an older child or an adult typically does, nor should she or he be influenced to do so. Nevertheless, a very young child does need help to realize what has happened and to make the emotional transition from life with a loved one to life without that person.

When death claims someone near and dear to your child, here are some suggestions for making that realization and transition easier:

■ Tell the truth about the death.

Children under six do not require lengthy medical or theological discussions about what death is like. They do need to be informed that their loved one has died and therefore won't be around anymore.

Saying that the deceased loved one has "gone away" without indicating that it's forever merely postpones the inevitable. Worse, your child will ultimately have a more difficult time accepting the death because of your well-meaning but confusing lie.

Saying that the loved one has "gone to sleep," even if you do indicate that it's forever, is also not advisable. It could make your child more fearful of sleep. This doesn't mean you can't *compare* death to sleep in terms of appearance and peacefulness.

Yet another problematic approach is to say that God took away the loved one. Your child might fear that she or he—or some other loved one—will be next, hopeless against the inscrutable workings of fate.

When you talk about the death, mention the general cause of death: sickness, injury, or old age. Again, details aren't necessary. What matters is that your child is not left completely in the dark. Depending on the maturity of your child—emotionally and intellectually—and on the nature of your relationship with each other, you may or may not choose to discuss details about the dying process or to reveal that a particular death was self-inflicted, murder, or the result of some catastrophe.

■ *Share your feelings about the death in an appropriate manner.*

Any death that has an emotional impact on your child will most likely have a similar impact on you. If the death involves someone very close, such as your spouse, your parent, or another child, it will have an especially strong and lasting effect on your behavior.

Emotionally intuitive as children are, your child will be aware of this impact on you whether you refer to it or not. The best policy, therefore, is to let your child know up front how you feel. It will make each of you feel less alone.

In expressing your emotions, be honest but ever mindful of your child's limited capacity to understand or share your reaction. You shouldn't frighten your child by appearing out of control or by using overly dramatic language (e.g., "I don't know how I'm going to keep on living"). However, you should prepare your child for the fact that you may not be functioning in quite the same way for a while.

■ *Allow your child to live her or his normal life as much as possible immediately after the death.*

Ideally, your child will be able to remain at home and engage in the predictable round of daily activities that provide an ongoing sense of security. This will minimize any fear your child may have that the death is going to alter her or his world in a radical way.

If the ideal is not possible, do whatver you reasonably can to make day-to-day life for your child the same as it was before the death. Mention the death to day-care workers, teachers, and any other adults who regularly interact with your child. Inform them that you want your child's normal routines maintained as much as possible.

■ *Offer your child some formal means of acknowledging the death and saying good-bye to the departed loved one.*

If the person who has died was very close to your child, and if it's at all practical, your child should attend the funeral so that she or he can feel like a part of the community of people who mourn the death. Don't burden your child, however, with a role in the funeral that is overly demanding.

In addition, try to arrange a more personal ceremony for your child to provide an outlet for any privately distressing feelings harbored about the death. Consider having a few minutes of silence together, saying a prayer, planting a tree in honor of the deceased, or visiting the grave. Check your local library and bookstores for material that suggests consoling activities for very young children who have recently lost a loved one.

■ If possible, allow a reasonable amount of time for the child to get over the death before introducing any major change into her or his life.

It's best not to take your child on a long trip, enroll your child in a new day-care center, or invite friends or family members to make extensive visits until at least a few weeks have passed and you've been able to determine that your child is accepting the death well. When a pet dies, put off getting a new one for at least a few weeks.

Very young children do tend to recover from a bereavement faster than older children and adults. But you don't want to rush the process or frustrate it by introducing yet another stressful event into their lives before they are emotionally ready for it.

7.

Separation Anxiety

Around six to nine months of age, children begin to recognize, cognitively and emotionally, that their parents are separate beings who may leave their company for extended periods of time. No longer does the absence of a parent simply inspire a fear in a child that her or his needs might not be met. From that point until the child is around two to three years old, it can trigger what psychology terms "separation anxiety"—the fear of losing the bond to the parent as an individual.

Separation anxiety can take many forms, but it generally involves clinging to the parent, crying when the parent leaves, and behaving poorly for at least a short time while she or he is away. It can occur when a mother or father leaves the room for a few minutes or the home for hours, days, or weeks at a time.

Separation anxiety is a particularly common problem when the ongoing, day-to-day relationship between parent and child is suddenly altered by new demands that the parent be elsewhere on a regular basis: most notably, when a mother returns to work after caring for her infant child full-time.

Sometimes separation anxiety manifests itself as a fear of "outsiders," a category that may not only include strangers but also close relatives, like grandparents, who don't live in the home. Children wrestling with this type of separation anxiety aren't as much afraid of the outsider as they are of the possibility that she or he might come between them and their parents.

Not all children under the age of three go through *observable* periods of separation anxiety, but most likely all of them do, in fact, experience it to some degree from time to time. If your child seems troubled by it, rest assured that it is a normal response and try managing it in the following ways:

■ *Prepare in advance for separations.*
If you'll be away for several hours or more, inform your child well in advance when, why, and how you will be leaving. Spend your last ten or fifteen minutes at home with your child. Don't leave as soon as the

caretaker arrives; let your child get used to her or his presence—and connnection to you—before you go.

■ Talk about what you'll do together when you return.

This will give your child something pleasant to anticipate that's associated with your leaving. The more specific you can be about what you'll do, the better, because the image in your child's mind will be sharper. Just make sure that you live up to your promise and do so as soon as possible after you are reunited.

■ Create a ritual way of leaving and returning.

For example, say the same special "good-bye" phrase every time you leave (preferably the last thing you do) and "hello" phrase every time you return (preferably the first thing you do). The predictability and special attention associated with such a ritual will be reassuring to your child.

■ Expect some initial distress.

You can't hope to eliminate separation anxiety entirely. It's an important stage in your child's development of a more mature, less stressful attachment to you. Therefore, be careful about communicating to your child that separation anxiety is wrong, upsetting, or intolerable. Above all, don't be unduly concerned yourself if your child exhibits more (or less!) anxiety on a particular occasion than you had anticipated.

■ Don't allow your own separation anxiety to feed the child's.

Don't make too big a deal out of how much you'll miss your child. You may be teaching your child to lament the separation even more severely than she or he already does.

Parents are especially prone to experience separation anxiety of their own when the tables are turned and their child must first leave home for an extended period of time—for example, to go to day care or nursery school. Avoid making such a transition more difficult for your child by putting off leaving your child behind, oversentimentalizing the occasion, or behaving noticeably in a different manner from the way you normally behave.

■ Prepare "strangers" for a potentially poor reception from your child.

Talk to people who will be visiting your home—or taking care of your child—about your child's separation anxiety and the shyness and fearfulness it may cause. Encourage these visitors and caretakers to avoid sudden gestures or overly close contact (such as a kiss or hug) until the child invites it or initiates it.

■ *If you'll be separated for several days or more, make audio-tapes or videotapes for your child.*

From time to time in your absence, these tapes can be played to reassure your child of your presence in the world and your continuing affection. Try reading aloud a favorite book, telling a family story, or talking about what you'll be doing while you're away.

■ *Practice miniseparations.*

One reason children in this age range love games like "now you see me, now you don't" or hide-and-seek is that they help them deal with their separation anxiety. They demonstrate that someone who "disappears" will in time "reappear."

In addition to such games, experiment with getting out of the house alone from time to time to perform short errands, leaving your child in the care of a neighbor, friend, or relative. The longer span of time that occurs between parent-child separations, the greater the anxiety will be when the next separation occurs.

CASE:

A Slice of the Other Life

Although Angie's father had always worked away from home during the weekdays, it wasn't until she was three years old that her mother began working in an office instead of at home. At first, the mother-and-daughter reunion at 5:00 P.M. was so happy and exciting for both of them that Angie didn't communicate the separation anxiety she felt during the day and her mother didn't suspect it. After a couple of weeks, however, Angie began exhibiting signs of sullenness and resentment at these reunions. Meanwhile, her reluctance to let her mother go in the morning was increasing rather than decreasing. It was clear to her mother that Angie was having problems accepting her absence.

Angie had visited her mother's office before, but only for a few minutes at a time. One evening, a television show gave Angie's mother an idea: If Angie could spend a sizable amount of time at the office every week or two, not only observing what her mother did there but also doing something there herself, it might help relieve her anxiety.

The following Saturday, Angie's mother brought Angie to her office. They were alone there, free to use their time as they wished. Angie's mother did some work of her own—routine work so that she could keep her eye on Angie—while Angie drew pictures and played with some of the safer office supplies and furniture. After two hours, they went out and had lunch together at a restaurant.

Angie's symptoms of separation anxiety quickly abated once she had developed a well-informed mental picture of her mother working at the office and in fact had "worked" there a few times herself. Angie realized that she could go to the office only on weekends, and only on those weekends that weren't otherwise busy. But with these occasional visits to anticipate, she was content to lead her independent day life from Monday through Friday.

8.
Discipline:
An Overview

In the context of child rearing, the word "discipline" still conjures up a Dickensian image of a stern, stiff-lipped adult shaking a hickory stick over an indignant, pouty-lipped child. The true meaning of the word is quite different. Discipline refers to the education of a novice (a "disciple"). Since a child is definitely a novice in life, the proper goal of discipline in child rearing is not *controlling* a child's behavior but *teaching* a child to control her or his own behavior.

In disciplining a child during the early years, adults need to remain ever aware that punishment in itself—or the threat of it—is a very poor deterrent to bad behavior. It's much more likely to breed resentment than to inspire good behavior. And although a resentful child may temporarily be a more cooperative child, she or he is almost certain to be a more estranged and devious one as well.

The first and foremost rule in disciplining a very young child is to be patient. Before you take any action, make sure you clarify in your own mind what you really want to accomplish as a result of that action.

For example, suppose you catch your child drawing on the wall with crayons. Your first thought may be: I want to put a stop to this right now! However, a moment's pause may help you appreciate that what you really want is to influence your child to respect family property and to associate the desire to draw with the right materials. If you scold your child too hastily or too harshly for making the walls dirty, you may thwart these goals. Knowing that drawing on the walls upsets you so much, your child may eventually do it again to strike back at you or, even worse, develop inhibitions about drawing or similar forms of creative self-expression.

A much better course of disciplinary action in this situation, given your goals, would to state strongly but more calmly that drawing *is* a good thing to do but that it is *not* good at all to draw on a wall.

Then you should make sure to involve your child in cleaning the wall and in imagining more appropriate drawing surfaces. Perhaps you'll find your child most enjoys drawing while standing up, in which case you can set up an easel for drawing or tape drawing paper to a special, out-of-the-way wall.

A different, more authoritative kind of disciplinary strategy is necessary to prevent your child from doing something dangerous. Suppose, for example, that you don't want your child to run into the street in front of your house. Your goal in this situation is not so much to encourage your child to behave in a more acceptable manner as it is to ensure that she or he does what you say. While you should certainly explain to your child *why* you want her or him to stay away from the street, your explanation alone may not bring about the result that you really want. The danger may be too theoretical for your child to appreciate; and if you make the danger too vivid, she or he may become unduly afraid of playing outdoors.

In this situation, it's better to insist earnestly that your child agree to the rule of not going into the street, thus making obedience rather than self-chosen behavior the focus of your discipline. The risk that your child may not obey you is too high to allow much leeway for failure, forgetfulness, or rebellion.

Besides underscoring the seriousness of a rule, you should repeat the rule often so that your child is sure to remember it. Creating a "rhyme" for a serious rule also helps. To keep your child from playing in the street, for example, you might formulate the rule "Keep your feet / Out of the street."

Assuming that you reserve such a disciplinary strategy—strict obedience to a rule—for circumstances that truly warrant it, you should have little difficulty getting your child to cooperate with it. She or he will realize that a demand so unusually strong must be very serious indeed. If you abuse this strategy by using it too often, it quickly becomes worthless.

Always taking time to consider the goals behind your disciplinary actions and commands will help you stay calm and collected during tense parent-and-child situations. It will also help you avoid mistreating your child unintentionally. Even the most conscientious parents can fall into the habit of issuing too many commands that are not at all in their child's interest but, rather, in their own. Consider, for example, a mother who tells her four-year-old daughter, "Hurry up and get ready," when she wants her child to accompany her on an errand. Is the mother acting in her daughter's interest or her own?

By itself, the mother's command is fairly innocuous, but it betrays a casual thoughtlessness that parents have to learn to keep in check, especially during moments when they are very angry with their child.

Parents can all too easily take for granted their love for, and authority over, their child. When this happens, they wind up confusing their wishes with what is best for their child. Meanwhile, their child winds up even more confused and possibly hurt and resentful as well.

For your own sake, or for the sake of your family, you may have to insist from time to time that your child do something that is not in her or his interest. Just be sure that you're aware of this fact when the occasion arises, that you reflect your awareness in your interaction with your child, that you offer a simple explanation for your request, and that you keep such occasions to a minimum. This way, your child will eventually learn to respect other people's interest as well as her or his own.

Here are some other ways to discipline very young children without causing counterproductive emotional problems:

■ Be clear, consistent, and dependable in applying discipline.

In many cases, the motive behind a very young child's misbehavior is a subconscious desire for order. The world as the child sees it is vastly mysterious and therefore threatening. To make matters worse, children at this age can't even depend on their own bodies or minds to do what they want them to do. Through their misbehavior, they cry out for their parents to set things right.

As a parent, it is your full-time responsibility to set firm standards of behavior for your child, to check periodically to make sure that your child understands and accepts those standards, and to function in a safely predictable way to maintain those standards. If you scream at your child for stealing cookies one day, only to smile indulgently when the same thing happens the next day, your child won't learn to control this behavior. Convinced that stealing sometimes might work, she or he will continue to leave the task of controlling to you.

If you live in a two-parent household, it's important for both you and your mate to use the same disciplinary style and to share disciplinary responsibilities in an equitable manner. Above all, one parent should never pass along the role of disciplinarian to the other parent, or bargain over who gets that role, in front of the child. Other people who may be responsible for disciplining your child, such as grandparents and baby-sitters, should be informed of the disciplinary measures you prefer and should be encouraged to use them.

■ Never discipline children by physically striking them.

Spanking or slapping a child is a signal that you've lost control of yourself. In essence, you're teaching a child that there are times when reason doesn't work and only brute force does. Out of fear, a child may temporarily respond to the physical assault with more acceptable behavior. The net result is certain to be latent resentment, increased emotional estrangement from the attacker, and eventual retaliation in some form or another.

The bond between a parent and a very young child is so emotionally volatile and the interactions that typically occur between them so potentially stressful that even the kindest and most loving parents can sometimes be tempted to spank or slap their children. This is particularly true when a child does something reckless that scares a parent, such as running around with a knife or accidentally starting a fire. An isolated instance of spanking or slapping, regrettable as it may be, is forgivable. Repeated reliance on spanking or slapping as a disciplinary technique is not.

As soon as you feel the impulse to strike or grab your child, try some tension-reducing strategy like counting to ten or insisting that you and your child sit down and remain quiet for a few seconds. If you do strike or grab your child in a moment of strong emotion, be patient with both yourself and the child. Explain why you acted the way you did and apologize.

■ Focus on the problem at hand, appealing to reason as much as possible.

A common mistake in disciplining children when they've broken a rule or created a problem is to complain about *them* instead of the *situation*. When you catch your very young son tearing pages out of a book, resist the tendency to blurt out, "Bad boy!" or, "Why are you always getting into trouble!" Instead, tell (or remind) him that it's a rule not to tear pages out of books and secure (or resecure) his agreement to that rule. He should also be made to deal with the consequences of his act. Instead of punishing him by not letting him watch television, which won't seem logical to him, insist that he clean up the mess he has made.

A more subtle form of attacking the child rather than the problem is merely *commanding* the child, instead of *teaching* her or him, to do—or not to do—something. For example, if your daughter is tormenting the family cat, it's much more constructive to say, "The cat can get hurt when you grab its legs like that," than it is to yell, "Don't bother the cat!"

■ When appropriate, use "time-out" as a disciplinary technique.

There are inevitably going to be situations when a very young child simply will not stop misbehaving. Regardless of what the parent says or does, the child will continue whining, running around the room, or knocking things off shelves. Most likely, the child is seeking whatever attention she or he can get, even if it's negative. In this type of situation, time-out can be a very effective disciplinary strategy.

Time-out involves telling a misbehaving child to go to a specific, isolated place and stay there until ready to behave in a more acceptable manner. This not only removes the child from the situation that is inspiring bad behavior but also gives the child a chance to appreciate, at a self-regulated pace, what she or he has lost by the bad behavior, that is, the company of others.

For consistency's sake, the time-out place should always be the same—a specific chair in a quiet place, or the child's room. If the child tends to return not yet ready to behave, a timer should be set for a minimum-required time-out period. Try starting with one minute for each year of age. Don't go beyond a thirty-minute maximum. A "time out" period shouldn't be too long, or it loses its effectiveness.

■ *If possible, offer alternatives rather than simply saying no.*
Suppose, for example, that your child is drumming on one of your pans. If you don't want the pan to be used that way, offer a more appropriate alternative to a drum. If the noise bothers you, suggest that your child drum outside. Or you might try proposing another activity altogether, such as drawing or playing with blocks. Limit yourself to offering just *two* choices, however. Otherwise, your child may get confused.

■ *Try to mix praise with blame, good news with bad news.*
Very young children can't accept discipline gracefully or constructively unless they are confident that you still love them and that life isn't going to be miserable forever as a result of what has happened. Remember, from a very young child's perspective, whatever she or he has done seemed to be the right thing to do at the time. If you refute this, then the child starts doubting everything.

There are several ways you can give your child the reassurance she or he needs without defeating your disciplinary purpose:

> ■ Be careful not to overdramatize the damage that's been done. For example, if your child empties all your dresser drawers on the floor, don't say, "It will take me all day to put this room back together," when it won't.

> ■ Invoke the child's "better self" whenever she or he misbehaves, either to help ensure that the bad behavior isn't repeated (e.g., "You always keep your promises to me, so I know I can count on you not to fight with your cousin again") or to let your child know that she or he has not lost your approval altogether (e.g., "I'm proud of the nice way you helped me out

this morning, but we have a rule about not playing with the curtains").

■ Refer to something pleasant that your child can anticipate (e.g., "I want you to pick up these scraps, and then you can play with your blocks").

■ *Apologize whenever you have done something wrong.*
Part of setting a good example for your very young child is being sure to apologize when you realize that you've done something wrong in the course of administering discipline. This includes wrongdoings such as accusing your child unjustly, contributing to the problem, not giving your child sufficient opportunity to explain or rectify her or his behavior, or punishing your child too harshly.

The most effective apology relating to a disciplinary situation is one that is immediate, short, and simple. Also, it should stand by itself. It doesn't need to be accompanied by any special treat to assuage your guilt.

Giving Orders That Work

You can prevent many of the behavioral problems exhibited by very young children—and improve the emotional climate of your parent-child relationship—by changing the way in which you issue your commands. Here are some suggestions:

■ *Make sure that your child can—and does—listen to you.*
Minimize or eliminate possible distractions (such as television noise), talk to your child face-to-face, and ask your child to repeat what you've said so that you can be certain that it has been understood.

■ *Don't phrase your command as a question.*
If you say, "Would you please stop hammering the floor?," you're inviting your child to say, "No." It's better to be more assertive: "Please stop hammering the floor."

■ *Avoid phrasing your command as a favor.*
Sometimes you will want to enlist your child's cooperation in doing something that's strictly for your own benefit. However,

try to limit the times when you refer to a command as a "favor." Children need to take it upon themselves to obey commands for their own benefit. Besides, if you make a practice of referring to commands as favors, your child may ultimately come to resent the imposition.

■ As often as possible, use the same particular tone of voice to issue commands.

Don't slip a command into your normal conversation with a very young child or experiment with a lot of indirect or cute ways of communicating a command. Be direct and use a tone of voice that is serious without being threatening.

■ Avoid issuing more than two commands at a time.

Very young children have a very limited attention span when it comes to conversations, not to mention a very limited tolerance for commands. If you stack several commands on top of each other, your child will feel overwhelmed. Even the child who can remember them all will most likely balk at fulfilling them.

■ If possible and appropriate, include an incentive in the command.

For example, instead of just saying, "It's time to get ready for bed," you could say, "It's time for you to go to bed, and then I can tell you a story"; or instead of just saying, "Please bring me that pot," you could say, "Please bring that pot to me so that I can start making your dinner." Avoid outright bribery. Also, be careful not to express yourself conditionally, for example, "If you'll pick up your clothes, we can start getting ready to go out." The use of "if" invites the child to comply or not to comply as she or he wishes.

■ Make sure that you stand behind your commands.

Don't let a child get away with refusing, forgetting, or deliberately failing to execute a command that you've given. Also, don't back down on the terms of a command unless your child offers very convincing reasons for you to do so. If your child absolutely refuses to cooperate, then you have no choice but to administer appropriate punishment.

How to Handle the "Gimmes" and the Grabs

Children under five can be very troublesome shopping companions, relentlessly begging for items that you don't want them to have or indiscriminately picking things off the shelves that catch their eye. As a result, what was intended to be a friendly outing together can turn into an emotionally exhausting tug-of-war for both of you.

Here are some suggestions for altering your child's unruly shopping behavior:

■ *Discuss the trip with your child ahead of time (at least ten minutes before you leave).*

Tell your child about what you're going to do together, what the experience will be like, and what kind of behavior you expect from her or him. This will give your child sufficient information and opportunity to get in the right mood.

■ *Before you enter the store, agree on one special thing your child can buy and stick to that agreement.*

To ensure that your child doesn't choose something inappropriate, you might want to ask her or him to select one among several stated options. Your child will feel more content to allow you to control the excursion knowing that she or he will derive specific and immediate gratification from it.

■ *Play a game as you go through the store.*

For example, give your child clues about what you want to buy next and ask her or him to guess what it is. Often the reason very young children are disruptive during a shopping trip is that they feel their parents are ignoring them.

■ *Offer your child an unexpected treat when you sense restlessness.*

Ideally, this treat will serve as a surprise reward for good behavior up to that point. If you're in a grocery store, consider offering your child something to be eaten during the rest of the time you are shopping.

■ *Give your child a specific amount of money to be spent as she or he wishes.*

This way, your child can feel independent, interested, and responsible instead of trapped, bored, and irresponsible. Whether or not this strategy is viable depends a great deal on how old, how careful, or how intellectually mature your child is. For a very young child, try simply stating the amount that can be spent. For an older child, try literally handing over the money.

■ *Engage your child as much as possible in helping you.*

Tell your child in advance what you want to get. Ask her or him to look for the next item you want. When the item has been located, ask your child to hand it to you. If both of you are legitimate shopping partners, your child will have a stronger emotional investment in making the experience a pleasant one.

Children age four through six may appreciate knowing how their parents make purchasing decisions. If so, their parents can simultaneously keep them occupied, foster their self-esteem, and educate them to be good consumers by involving them in choosing specific items: for example, the freshest fruit or the better of two different types of trash cans.

Managing Whining and Tantrums

The second year of a child's life is infamously known as the "terrible twos." At this age, children are just beginning to form independent identities and to realize that there can be an enormously frustrating gap between what they want of themselves, of their parents, and of the world and what they actually get.

To make matter worse, two-year-olds haven't yet mastered the language of adults. Unable to express in words exactly how they feel or to get the results they expect from the words they do use, they resort either to whining (a combination of "baby" crying and "adult" speaking) or to tantrums (a combination of "baby" helplessness and "adult" violence). In many cases, a frustrated child will employ both strategies, beginning with the milder one, whining, and building up to the more intense one, a tantrum—at which point the child quickly loses all fragile powers of self-control.

Unfortunately, this pattern of bad behavior doesn't come to an end when the child turns three. The typical reign of terror for whining lasts until the child is around three and a half years old, and the typical reign of terror for tantrums frequently lasts until the child is around four and a half years old. Thereafter, incidents of whining and tantrums still occur, but much more sporadically, unless the child is suffering some especially strong emotional disturbance.

Because whining and tantrums are motivated in the same way, they can be managed by parents in the same way. To say that they can be managed doesn't mean that they can *always* be stopped or even that they can *usually* be stopped. Like a spell of bad weather, a spell of whining or tantrum throwing often must be simply endured with as much equanimity as one can muster. Nevertheless, here is a practical six-step approach that can help tame the terror:

1. Investigate.
Make sure that your child's whining or crying isn't the result of fatigue, hunger, discomfort, or illness. If one of these factors does seem to be responsible, take appropriate action.

2. Distract.
A child in the grip of a whining jag or a tantrum needs your help to snap out of it. Try to interest your child in something that you know she or he likes, such as a beloved toy or game.

3. Ignore.
If there's no physical reason behind the bad behavior or if you can't distract your child, the best strategy is simply to ignore the behavior, no matter how difficult doing so may be. Eventually, your child will realize she or he is not getting any results from the whining or the tantrum and will stop. The more you ignore the behavior, the less inclined your child will be to resort to it, which is, after all, likely to be much more stressful to your child than to you.

4. Isolate.
Leave your child alone or insist that your child take time-out in a place specifically designated for that purpose (e.g., a quiet corner in the den or your child's room).

5. Record.

Keep a log of each time your child has a major whining fit or tantrum. You may discover that such behavior generally occurs at the same time of day, or in the context of the same type of activity. If so, you may be able to take action to forestall or eliminate future episodes of this behavior.

6. Teach.

Whenever possible—before, during, or after the incident of bad behavior—help your child learn more acceptable behavior for getting what she or he wants, or for passing the time when she or he is bored, sad, or out of sorts.

QUESTIONNAIRE:

Your Child's Self-Discipline

For each general situation listed below, rate your child's typical, overall behavior on a scale of 1 to 5: 1 indicating no discipline problems and 5 indicating a frequent occurrence of extremely defiant and unruly behavior. If you have difficulty completing this questionnaire or would first like to monitor your child's situational behavior more closely, photocopy this questionnaire and complete it at the end of a two-week or monthlong period of observation.

When you've completed the questionnaire, focus on the situations that you've rated 3 or higher and work on making them less troublesome. Take special note of any patterns that emerge, such as several poor ratings involving behavior when other people are around or compliance with requests. If you've given a rating of 3 or more to over twelve of the twenty-five situations listed, consider seeking professional help.

		PROBLEM FREQUENCY			
	low				high
1. During meals	1	2	3	4	5
2. While getting up in the morning	1	2	3	4	5
3. During the morning (in general)	1	2	3	4	5

	PROBLEM FREQUENCY				
	low				high
4. During the afternoon (in general)	1	2	3	4	5
5. During the evening (in general)	1	2	3	4	5
6. At bedtime	1	2	3	4	5
7. Overnight (while in bed)	1	2	3	4	5
8. While the television is on	1	2	3	4	5
9. While playing alone	1	2	3	4	5
10. While playing with other children	1	2	3	4	5
11. While alone with mother	1	2	3	4	5
12. While alone with father	1	2	3	4	5
13. While with a baby-sitter	1	2	3	4	5
14. While riding in the car	1	2	3	4	5
15. While visiting a public place	1	2	3	4	5
16. While getting dressed or undressed	1	2	3	4	5
17. During washing or bathing	1	2	3	4	5
18. While visitors are present	1	2	3	4	5
19. While visiting other homes	1	2	3	4	5
20. When asked to perform tasks	1	2	3	4	5
21. When you deny requests	1	2	3	4	5
22. When asked to change behavior or obey rules	1	2	3	4	5
23. While you're talking on the telephone	1	2	3	4	5
24. While you're focusing your affection on someone else (spouse, lover, other child, relative, best friend)	1	2	3	4	5
25. While you're absorbed in performing some task	1	2	3	4	5

CASE:

Nothing But the Truth

One hot summer afternoon, Debra and her best friend, Yvonne, took Cally, Debra's new five-year-old stepdaughter, to the zoo. After a couple of hours, Debra was exhausted. Cally, on the other hand, was still going strong. When Debra said, "It's time to go home," Cally started begging, "No, I don't want to go, I want to look at the lions." Reluctant to disappoint her step-daughter and risk jeopardizing their fragile relationship, Debra backed down and took Cally to the lion area.

Afterward, Debra again said, "It's time to go home," and met with further resistance. "No, no!" Cally pleaded. "We didn't see the baby chimp!" Completely frustrated, Debra snapped back, "Don't be a whiner, Cally. We've been here long enough. You either come with me, or I'm leaving you behind!" Cally plunked herself down on a nearby bench and pouted. Debra turned to Yvonne and asked in a low voice, "Now what do I do?"

Speaking from her own child-raising experiences, Yvonne replied, "Do what you'd do with me or anyone else. Be fair. Tell her what's really going on. Tell her you're tired, that you can come back some other time." Debra sat down next to Cally and admitted to her that she was tired. Cally jumped up and took her hand, and the three of them left the zoo with no more fuss.

CASE:

An Element of Surprise

Every now and then a parent can stop a tantrum in its tracks by resorting to some inspired zaniness as a distraction. Robby, age two and a half, was a frequent tantrum thrower. It usually worked to leave him alone—literally, by going into another room. But one Thanksgiving morning Robby burst into a major tantrum just as everyone was about to go to a family gathering across town. There wasn't any time to wait Robby out.

Acting on impulse, Robby's mother pulled her compact from her purse, put an arm firmly around his waist, and lightly powdered his hair and his stomach while making sounds like a bell: "Ring-a-ding-ding! Ring-a-ding-ding!" Dumbfounded, Robby abruptly ceased crying and thrashing around. In a few seconds, he was actually laughing at his mother's goofiness.

CASE:

Who's the Boss?

Bob and Leslie were at their wits' end in dealing with their three-year-old son, Craig. He seemed to be a born dictator, constantly issuing orders according to his wishes: "Do this!" "Come here!" "Stop that!" "Not now!" Bob and Leslie were assertive people themselves, capable of admiring Craig's masterful spirit to some degree, but not in the tyrannical form it appeared to be assuming. Every moment in his company was turning into a battle of wills.

Finally, Bob and Leslie consulted with a child psychiatrist. With the latter's help, they formulated their frustrations into a few key questions: Why was Craig's behavior so combative? How could they tolerate it in the short term? How could they work to change Craig's behavior in the long term so it would be less obnoxious?

First, Bob, Leslie, and the psychiatrist discussed Craig's personal, family, and home-life history, especially his recent, day-to-day experiences. They established that their son had always been rather strong-willed, that there weren't any other noteworthy problems in his history or home life, and that his recent day-to-day experiences in themselves were not remarkably different from those of a "normal" three-year-old. Then the psychiatrist spent several hours getting to know Craig and his parents better, both as individuals and as a family group. Ultimately, they arrived at some answers to the key questions they had posed.

Why was Craig's behavior so combative? In essence, it is typical for three-year-olds to engage in battles of the will. It's a matter of testing and proving one's newly emerging strength to oneself and everyone else. In Craig's case, this development was compounded by his basic temperament, an assertive one that wasn't negative in itself but did require special handling. A contributing factor in his behavior was the basically assertive temperaments of his parents, who were naturally predisposed to view each troublesome interaction with Craig as a "win-lose" struggle.

How could Bob and Leslie tolerate Craig's behavior in the short term? Above all, they realized that they needed to learn more about child development at different ages so they could be more compassionate about the possible age-related strengths and weaknesses that were influencing their son's behavior. They also determined to prepare for each day more carefully. Their daily planning goal would be to avoid confrontational situations as much as possible and to maximize times when the three of them would be the most capable of enjoying each other's company.

How could they work to change Craig's behavior in the long term so that it would be less obnoxious? They decided that the best strategy was to "give in" gracefully to Craig's demands whenever possible—that is, when nothing really important was at stake. At the same time, they would gently make sure that Craig used polite language in his demands, like "please" and "thank you."

At times when it was necessary for Craig to cooperate with their wishes, Bob and Leslie would try not to *demand* cooperation, given Craig's unusually strong, combative nature. Instead, they would casually stage-manage the situation so that Craig would be maneuvered to cooperate without having to lose face. For example, instead of saying, "Get in the car, Craig, I want you to go to the store with me," in which case Craig would be challenged to refuse, they would say, "Okay, Craig, we're going to the store now" as they headed straight for the car, in which case Craig would be more inclined to follow along.

Also, Bob and Leslie made a special effort to leave Craig alone more frequently with a male baby-sitter—a teenager in the neighborhood who had earned their trust, who liked children, and who was very fair yet firm in dealing with them. An assertive child like Craig often profits from being around older kids and adults, especially of the same sex. They have the experience to temper the child's combativeness in a constructive manner, plus they provide a same-sex model for more mature interactive behavior.

At PCGC: Treatment in a Family Context

Children under six who have severe disciplinary or behavioral problems can't be separated from their parents for extensive treatment without suffering some degree of trauma. Furthermore, a very young child's disciplinary and emotional problems are most effectively analyzed by examining that child in the context of her or his family life rather than in the context of an isolating, institutional testing.

One solution to these difficulties is to offer a "home-living" environment within the hospital or clinic: a place where the family can remain together and function as a family while the child's problems are being evaluated. This situation allows clinicians and treatment teams to witness the family culture in operation—either through "visits" or through one-way mirror observation—and to apply systematically a variety of interventions in a controlled environment.

In addition to severe disciplinary and behavioral problems, issues involving very young children that are appropriate for this kind of comprehensive on-site care include:

■ emotional complications relating to a chronic physical illness;

■ psychosomatic disorders, such as asthma, gastrointestinal illness, or diabetes;

■ a situation where there are multiple patients within a single family.

PCGC has a "Family Apartment Unit Program" that offers this kind of clinical approach for very young children and their families needing intensive psychiatric evaluation and treatment in a therapeutic setting. The family as a whole literally moves into a two-room apartment (bedroom and living room/dining and kitchen area) within the PCGC complex for professional observation and intervention on a twenty-four-hour basis.

Prior to admission of the family, there are several assessment conferences with the family and the referring therapist to clarify how the program runs and how it might be useful and to arrange a schedule for the program that suits all individuals involved. On arrival at the apartment for participation in the program, the family inevitably has to mobilize its resources to cope with the novel circumstances. This effort in itself helps move the family toward positive change.

Once the family is fairly well established in the apartment, PCGC clinicians and treatment teams orchestrate therapeutic interventions to correspond with their observations. A "typical" family therapy session is only one of many possible interventions aimed at reorganizing the way the family functions so that it as a whole and the child in particular can better manage the latter's problem. Other possibilities include testing (medical as well as psychological), education, conflict resolution, skill training, role-playing, and behavioral modification.

The primary considerations for discharge from PCGC's Family Apartment Unit Program are whether there has been a decrease in the child's symptoms and whether the family has begun to show itself capable of modifying those patterns of interaction that contribute to the child's problem. The overall goal in every case is for the family to learn how to take effective control of its own difficulties and how to make effective use of outside support systems.

Look for programs like PCGC's Family Apartment Unit Program in your area. If none exist, consult with your psychiatrist, psychologist, or mental-health professional about incorporating similar features into your child's therapy.

9.

Toilet Training

Few issues cause as much tension between parents and their very young children as toilet training. Fairly or unfairly, parents can't help but approach this disciplinary challenge not only as a test of their child's temperament and intelligence but also as a means of releasing them from singularly unpleasant and time-consuming cleanup responsibilities. No wonder there are so many misconceptions regarding when and how to meet this challenge!

Let's look at some of the major toilet-training myths and test them against reality:

■ *Myth #1: There is a proper age at which to train a child to use a toilet.*

Children need to be both physically and cognitively ready for controlling elimination, and each child achieves this readiness at her or his own pace. Seldom does this occur before eighteen months of age, so attempting to train a child any earlier is almost certain to lead to frustration and conflict for all parties concerned. Most children are ready sometime between the ages of two and four.

■ *Myth #2: You'll know for sure when to begin toilet training.*

Unfortunately, there is no one clear signal that all the brain-to-body connections have been made and all the emotional maturity has been developed that will enable your child to respond favorably to toilet training. You must make this judgment based on close observation of your child's daily behavior.

Among the clues that your child *may* be ready for toilet training are the following:

> ■ Your child indicates the need to eliminate, either verbally or nonverbally (e.g., by clutching self, going red in the face, crossing the legs), *in advance*.

> ■ Your child shows concern about her or his elimination habits or your reaction to them.

■ Your child chooses to watch—and perhaps imitate—your elimination habits.

■ Your child expresses discomfort about wearing diapers and/or eliminating in them.

■ Your child is independently capable of getting into, and out of, loose-fitting pants.

■ *Myth #3: There is one right way to toilet train a child.*
In each case, toilet training is essentially a trial-and-error proposition. Some children train quickly (e.g., in a couple of weeks); others don't. Some make steady progress; others go through several periods of retreat. Still others defy classification: All methods may seem to fail for months in a row, until suddenly the desired behavior falls into place.
Here are some general guidelines for toilet training your child:

■ Well before training starts, teach your child about the parts of the body involved in elimination and how they function. This teaching doesn't need to be elaborate and shouldn't be judgmental. It's simply a matter of helping your child learn more about her or his body on a casual, day-to-day basis. Your child should also become familiar with the toilet and the potty well before she or he is expected to use them.

■ Assist your child in self-training rather than merely imposing a training program. When your child gives a verbal or nonverbal clue of the need to eliminate, suggest that she or he do so in the potty. Try not to insist if you encounter strong resistance to this suggestion.
    Children tend to be fairly predictable in their elimination habits (e.g., needing to move their bowels after eating breakfast). Take note of such patterns and help your child to prepare for easy use of the potty or toilet at appropriate times (e.g., by postponing diapering or suggesting that she or he sit on the potty at these times and play with a special potty-only toy). Don't compel a child to eliminate when she or he has not indicated a readiness.

■ Avoid dramatic reactions, one way or the other, to your child's training. Don't be overly enthusiastic when your child succeeds. Simply compliment her or him on being so grown up. Upon failure, suggest that the potty or toilet be tried the next time. These tempered reactions will keep your child from associating toilet training with volatile emotions.
    As much as possible, try not to refer to success in using the potty or toilet as "good" and failure as "bad." Also, avoid la-

beling the products of elimination as "disgusting." These terms are judgmental and confuse the goal of training, which is not to learn new *values* but to master a new *skill*.

■ *Myth #4: Children are forever traumatized by inappropriate toilet training.*

Daunting as it may seem to the parent at the time and despite popular folklore, toilet training is *not* the most significant determinant of a child's future psychological health. As long as the training is not abusive or linked to a stringent punishment-and-reward system, there shouldn't be any negative psychological aftereffects.

■ *Myth #5: When bed-wetting occurs after toilet training, the cause is some emotional disturbance.*

Regardless of a child's emotional state, occasional, uncontrollable bed-wetting can persist beyond otherwise successful toilet training as late as seven years of age. Bed-wetting can also cease for long periods of time and then resume.

Bed-wetting

In most cases, a combination of factors are responsible for bed-wetting beyond toilet training: developmental (e.g., immature bladder capacity, often inherited and almost always outgrown); medical (due to such rare problems as a urinary tract infection); situational (e.g., overtiredness resulting in deeper sleep); and/or emotional (e.g., going to bed in a state of overexcitement or anxiety, which may stimulate bladder release).

Contrary to popular folklore, bed-wetting for children under seven is seldom strictly emotional in origin. And the emotions that do seem to be involved in certain bed-wetting cases are very generalized ones rather than specific emotions that can be associated with particular psychological issues.

If your very young child indicates that she or he is upset or ashamed by bed-wetting, offer gentle reassurance that such things happen and that no one is to blame. You might also tell the child that you will keep this incident a secret, since it is a private matter. Your child may be afraid that other members of the family will find out.

A Natural Transition

Rita sensed that her two-and-a-half-year-old son, Cruz, might be ready for toilet training when he told her that he didn't like his grandmother changing his diapers. That he even mentioned his diapers suggested to Rita that he might be interested in an alternative. She encouraged Cruz to become more familiar with the potty and to ask to use it whenever he felt the need, but this approach wasn't very successful. Rarely did Cruz ask to have his diaper removed so that he could go to the potty.

Finally, during a monthlong period when Rita was off work, she decided it was worth risking some messy moments to let Cruz have the full experience of life without diapers. She put him in training pants and hoped for the best. The first time urine ran down Cruz's leg, he was amazed and curious. The second time, he was plainly displeased. He began right away to be better at using the potty.

Nevertheless, Cruz didn't convert to the potty completely until the day when he spent an afternoon with his mother at a nearby playground. After an hour of swinging, climbing, and sliding, he was still eager for more. Then, suddenly, he had a bowel movement in his pants. He immediately realized, in a very visceral way, that this meant having to go home to clean up instead of playing. He never let such a thing happen again.

10.
Siblings:
Old and New

In all multichild households, there are inevitably major differences between the way parents see the relationships among their children and the way their very young children see them. Although parents can't help but nourish visions of their offspring as an essentially loving team or community, their very young children see themselves first and foremost as solitary beings. And while parents strive to remain always aware of each child's individual personality, needs, desires, and rights, their very young children are inclined to pull in the opposite direction—that is, to focus attention on their own specific personality, needs, desires, and rights. These widely divergent points of view make friction between very young children and their siblings especially difficult for parents to understand and manage.

First, let's consider the basic kinds of sibling conflicts that children under six experience. Then we can look at ways to deal with each one. The sibling conflicts most likely to affect children in this age range can be divided into three main categories:

1. The child argues with a sibling over a specific possession, judgment, or privilege.

This happens from time to time in every household with more than one child. The *apparent* cause of a particular argument may be gaining custody of a toy, occupying a specific sitting place, choosing a television program, defining the conditions of a game, establishing who is right, defending one's privacy, or simply gaining control of a parent's attention. A *hidden* cause of the argument may be one child's (or both children's) fatigue, hunger, or negative response to a temporarily stressful situation in the household (e.g., a visit by an outsider). An additional problem resulting from the argument may be physical violence, name-calling, or intense emotional frustration, manifesting itself in crying, withdrawal, or a tantrum.

2. The child is generally and consistently abusive to—or abused by—a sibling.

This situation is much less common than the one described above. It seldom gives rise to a two-party argument. Instead, one child is always the quick and clear perpetrator; the other, the victim.

Sometimes this is merely due to one child's being markedly more aggressive in temperament than the other. It may, however, be the result of a more specific issue. The perpetrator may be convinced that she or he continually receives an unfairly small or inferior share of possessions, privileges, or attention compared to the other child. Or the perpetrator may be reacting negatively to an ongoing stressful situation in the household, such as entrenched marital discord, by repeatedly taking out related frustrations on the easiest target.

3. The child fears being abandoned by the parents in favor of a new child.

It is quite common for a child under six years old to become upset at the prospect—or arrival—of a new brother or sister. This is especially true if she or he is an only child.

Normal symptoms of such a reaction (which is fundamentally an *adjustment* reaction, not a *denial* reaction) include recurring anxiety, moodiness, anger, withdrawal, and/or regression, a condition in which the child reverts to immature and even babyish behavior. Sometimes the child will take out ill feelings on the baby; other times, on the parent; much less often, on another child in the family. Almost always, however, the ill feelings have to do with a fear of losing the parents' affection, not with actual hatred for the baby.

Here are some suggestions for managing each of the above-mentioned categories of sibling conflict:

1. Your child argues with a sibling over a specific possession, judgment, or privilege.

■ *Discuss the situation in the presence of both children.*

If you actually witness the argument, you may want to intervene directly and immediately, depending on the age of the participants and the nature of the quarrel. For example, if your three-year-old daughter is unfairly bullying her two-year-old sister, you should gently but firmly clarify for both children's benefit what is right and wrong about the situation and then secure your three-year-old's promise to behave more fairly. Assuming your quarreling children are both in the four- to six-year-old range, you might be able to take the less authoritative role of moderator, assisting your children in discussing the problem with you and realizing for themselves what would be a fair solution.

If you don't witness the argument, be sure that both children come together in your presence before you begin to discuss what happened. Listen to each child in turn and then guide them to work out a problem-solving agreement in the most appropriate manner, according to the age and maturity of both children.

■ *If your children won't cooperate in discussing or resolving the problem, impose separation and time-out.*
Make sure that your children retire to—and remain in—separate rooms and that they have the time and tranquillity to think about what has happened. In some cases, this is an especially strong and instructive punishment. Difficult as it may be for a parent to appreciate, the two children may, in fact, have been expressing their enjoyment of being together by fighting. In such cases, the issue is not so much to get the two children to enjoy each other's company *more* but to get them to do so *in a more appropriate manner*.

■ *Keep track of the arguments that erupt between the two children and use this information to forestall, prevent, or manage future arguments.*
Among the items to monitor are when each argument happens, why it happens, what is going on in the life of each child at that time, what is going on in the life of the household at that time, what helps to resolve the argument, and what doesn't help.

---

2. Your child is generally and consistently abusive to—or abused by—a sibling.
In addition to applying the guidelines for the previous category to each particular incident, take the following steps:

■ *Examine your ongoing home life very carefully for any factor that may be causing or aggravating this situation.*
Among the questions you should ask yourself are the following: Am I giving each child an equal amount of high-quality, individual attention? Has the family been going through a difficult period of time lately (e.g., due to marital discord, tough work schedules, economic adversity, or prolonged and serious illness)? Has either child been going through a difficult period of time lately (e.g., due to a change in daily routine, a new stage in physical development, or new people in her or his daily environment)?

If you feel that any of these factors is causing or aggravating sibling conflict, then do what you can to diminish, remove, or alleviate its impact.

■ *Seek professional advice.*

Interpersonal behavior that is consistently negative can be a sign of a deeply rooted problem either in the emotional makeup of the child or in family dynamics. Even if it's not, the price of letting it continue for longer than a few months is just too great. It can jeopardize not only the future emotional health of the two children directly involved but also that of every family member.

3. Your child fears being abandoned by you in favor of a new child.

■ *Prepare your child in advance to have informed and realistic expectations about the newborn.*

Among the things to do are the following: Explain to your child how the baby was conceived, how the baby is going to develop, and what the baby will be like for the first few months after birth. Involve your child in some of the prenatal activities (e.g., weighing your child whenever you weigh yourself or shopping for baby goods). Try to let your child observe other newborns, preferably as you handle them, so that she or he will know what to expect and what not to expect.

Among the things *not* to do: Don't emphasize how much your child will enjoy the new baby, since this may not be the case. Don't characterize the baby as a "new playmate," since your child won't really be able to—and, in fact, should not—play with the baby for some time after the birth. Don't impress upon the child that you will need help in taking care of the baby, since she or he may not be capable of—or interested in—providing the help you really need.

■ *Spend additional time alone with your child in advance of the birth.*

This will reaffirm your child's place in your heart as well as in your daily schedule. Take advantage of this time to recall and review your child's personal history with the family. It will reinforce her or his sense of being forever special. Look at old baby photos together and reminisce about favorite experiences.

■ *Try to include your child in the excitement surrounding the baby's birth.*

If possible, arrange to have your child visit you and the newborn in the hospital or hospice (an alternative-health-care facility). Record the first meeting of the child and her or his new sibling with a photograph, movie, or tape. Give your child a present for now being a big sister or a big brother and encourage friends and relatives to give your child a present at the same time that they give a present to the new baby. (The two presents don't have to be equal in value.)

■ *As much as possible, avoid leaving your child alone with your new baby until the latter is around two years old.*
A child under six is very capable of unintentionally—or intentionally—hurting a younger child physically or emotionally, so it's best not to take any chances. Keep the two of them always in sight. Use a playpen whenever appropriate to guard your baby when the two of them are in the same room. Avail yourself of baby-sitters, day care, or nursery school to give your child appropriate time away from the baby and to give yourself appropriate time away from having to watch over the two of them at once. Also, try to stagger mealtimes, nap times, and bedtimes.

■ *Be sure to continue spending regular time alone with your child.*
Do things together that you've always done so that your child feels a sense of continuity. In addition, introduce new things to do so that your child feels newly stimulated by your relationship. While it's wise to devote a certain amount of time to activities that have nothing to do with the new baby, you might slowly interject appropriate baby-related projects, such as discussing with your child safe ways to interact with the baby.

CASE:

Like Baby, Like Mother

When four-and-a-half-year-old Diana was first told she was going to have a new sister or brother, she had only two questions: "How are babies made?" and "When will the baby be here?" For the next couple of months, she gave no signs of any reaction one way or another. Her parents kept reminding her that the baby was growing and would be there soon, but she didn't seem at all curious.

However, once her mother's pregnant state became visibly obvious, things changed. Formerly a very mature child for her age, she began regressing. The first indications were wetting her bed again—after eighteen months of no problems—and opting more often to crawl than to walk. Within a couple of weeks she was also demanding to be fed from a bottle and throwing an occasional tantrum when she didn't get her way.

Distressed as Diana's mother was by this behavior, she resisted the impulse to be angry at Diana for not acting her age.

Instead, she let her daughter do as she wished. She intervened only when absolutely necessary; and when she did, she treated Diana in about the same way she had when Diana had originally exhibited the behavior at a younger age.

Diana continued her regressive behavior for another three months, until about six weeks before the baby was due. Then, over the span of a single week, she did a complete turnabout. She began tending her favorite baby doll more solicitously than she ever had before, as if she were the new mother that her real mother was about to be. Her parents speculated that she had finally tired of living like an infant because it wasn't fun. Furthermore, it wasn't getting her the special attention she had imagined it might when she had observed her parents' eager anticipation of the new baby.

No longer did Diana wet her bed, crawl on the floor, feed from a bottle, or throw tantrums. Indeed, she played with her doll-child as if it were exhibiting those behaviors! When her new baby brother finally arrived home, she was behaving more maturely than she ever had, and the adjustment to her new sibling was much smoother than her parents had expected.

11.
Play

Play is the child's natural work. For very young children, it's their most valuable means of learning about themselves and the world around them. Powerless to do much more than *react* to adult supervision, they rely on playtime as their only opportunity to *act* as they wish; and this kind of self-determination is essential to their healthy development as human beings. Through play, children can teach themselves—safely, enjoyably, and instinctively—to appreciate their personal strengths and weaknesses, derive satisfaction from tasks and objects in their environment, and interact effectively with others.

In terms of emotional health, play offers very young children two particularly important benefits: First, it gives them a creative, instructive, and appropriate outlet for their feelings; second, it trains them to read the feelings of others and to respond to them in a socially acceptable manner.

Let's begin by considering how play functions as an emotional outlet. This process is observable in children as young as six months, when many babies first display an interest in peekaboo, a game that allows them to gain more control over the stress associated with a parent being "out of sight." A year or two later, children typically discharge feelings of anger, incompetence, and insecurity by building things with blocks and then tearing them down or by "acting out" such feelings in make-believe exchanges with dolls, stuffed animals, and action toys.

From around four or five years old, a child may start engaging in more violent forms of play: "pretend" fighting and even killing, especially boys. While such play may startle adult sensibilities, it is perfectly normal and even healthy for the children themselves. It guides them to discharge general feelings of hostility and vulnerability in a safely make-believe manner. Far from influencing children to become more belligerent in real life, "gunplay" (as such an activity is collectively called) can teach them to control their aggressive impulses. Psychologists often refer to this phenomenon as "reduction through symbolic play."

That aggressive play can be good for a child does not mean that parents should encourage it or refrain from regulating it when it becomes too rowdy. Nor does it mean that parents must ignore their own negative feelings about violence or war and play along with their children. Some children are more inclined toward this kind of activity—for all sorts of reasons—than others. Some are rowdier than others. And all of them need to get used to the fact that other people, including parents, are free to say yes or no when they're invited to play a particular game.

In your own household, the best strategy for coping with your child's occasional desire for violent play is first to make sure that she or he also has—or knows about—a number of interesting play options that are nonviolent. Then let your child play however she or he chooses, as long as it's safe and doesn't disturb others.

Here are some other suggestions regarding play:

■ *Give your child ample opportunities and resources for play, both alone and with others.*

As much as possible, build in regular, predictable times during your child's day when she or he is free to play alone. This will help your child become more independent. To increase your child's social skills, arrange regular, predictable "play dates" during the week with other children.

Also, do whatever you reasonably can to facilitate enjoyable play. Establish safe, roomy, and comfortable play areas in your home. Make sure to create play areas that you can easily observe as well as others that will allow each of you to have some degree of privacy. Help make sure that your child's toys are well organized so that different types are readily available for each given playtime. Take a variety of them along when you and your child are away from home in case a chance for play presents itself.

Play can be a wonderful solace when your child is emotionally troubled. Be alert for such times and gently lead your child by offering several attractive and appropriate play alternatives. For example, if your child feels neglected, you might propose playing together with dolls or playing Simon says—both very interactive games involving a great deal of personal attention.

■ *Regularly join your child in play.*

You and your child can develop a much closer bond if you know how to play together in a number of different ways and if you can depend on frequent play-together periods to communicate with each other—directly or indirectly. With this in mind, be sure to choose or devise a number of toys and games for your child that both of you are capable of enjoying.

■ *Be as patient as possible with your child's progress in mastering skills and learning to obey rules.*

Let your child take the lead, or have the feeling of taking it, when you play together. A child under six is often not emotionally equipped to handle losing very well, so be prepared to let your child win, even if it means allowing her or him to cheat. A certain amount of cheating may be necessary for your child to get through a game until she or he has acquired more proficiency, at which point the desire to cheat will most likely disappear.

■ *Tactfully help your child play well and gain maximum benefits from doing so.*

Without putting a damper on your child's fun, make her or him aware of the value of different games: what can be learned from them or how they can develop the body or mind. This information will help your child appreciate certain games more strongly. Then, when you play games with children, set a good example—and, if necessary, tailor the rules of the game—so that your child can derive maximum satisfaction from it.

Take care to play games with your child that suit her or his mood and the time of day. Relatively quiet games, for example, are more appropriate if your child is sad or listless or if it's almost bedtime. On the other hand, if your child is rambunctious and it's the middle of the afternoon, a more active game is appropriate.

At this stage in life, your child may have difficulty sharing toys with others or allowing them their fair turn. Gently establish what is right or nice as opposed to what is wrong or not nice and don't hesitate to intervene when necessary if your child is victimizing, or being victimized by, another child.

You might also try "practice sharing" rituals with your child, in which you ask to be given a toy, praise your child upon giving it to you, and then return it in a few seconds. However, don't expect your child to adopt more generous behavior very quickly and don't worry if she or he doesn't. It takes a considerable amount of time and experience for a child to recognize the value of sharing and fair play.

■ *Discreetly observe your child at play.*

Make a habit of watching your child play from time to time in a manner that doesn't attract attention. How or what your child plays can give you valuable insights into a host of current feelings. For example, your child may invent a frustrating scenario with a doll that you can relate to a specific troublesome scenario in her or his real life. Or your child may appear to have lost interest in some favorite toys, which could well signal a more complicated emotional conflict (such as separation anxiety). But even more important, routinely watching your child at play can tell you more about what she or he likes and dislikes. This knowledge will help you buy toys and plan playtimes that your child will enjoy and will ensure that you and your child have fun when you play together.

■ *Invite your child to bring a playful spirit to everyday activities.* Cleanup tasks, simple chores around the kitchen and yard, and daily rituals like bathtime can be made much more attractive and less stressful to your child if they are given a gamelike quality. Try accompanying such activities with playacting, sing-alongs, or follow-the-leader exercises. This kind of approach also allows your child to translate more easily into real life the skills acquired through play.

Group Games for the Early Years

Until kids are five or six years old, they are usually too self-centered to participate well in sustained games with other children. They lack the necessary concentration and cooperation skills, and they don't take losing gracefully. They do, however, love to play self-challenging games either in unison or by taking turns, especially if those games are structured around rhythm, repetition, or chanting.

Here are some specific group-game suggestions for different age ranges:

TWO TO THREE YEARS OLD

Children during these years are especially fond of games that exercise their newly emerging language and motor skills, like ring-around-a-rosy, mulberry bush, egg hunt, and follow the leader. As a rule, they are not yet emotionally mature enough for games with a strong acceptance-rejection theme (e.g., farmer in the dell, in which different players are chosen—or not chosen—to assume different roles).

THREE TO FIVE YEARS OLD

Children at this stage in their development enjoy a game that involves slightly more sophisticated motor skills. They are also emotionally mature enough for the game to include a mild degree of competition and/or acceptance-rejection. Ideal games of this nature include Simon says, hot and cold, London Bridge, bobbing for apples, pin the tail on the donkey, and musical chairs.

FIVE TO SIX YEARS OLD

By the time a child is age five or six, she or he is rapidly acquiring interpersonal skills and emotional resiliency. It's a good time for role-related games such as farmer in the dell, blindman's buff, hide-and-seek, cowboys and Indians, cops and robbers, relay racing, and leapfrog.

Imaginary Playmates

Anytime from age three and a half to age six, your child may go through one or more periods of having a make-believe friend: someone that your child openly includes in most daily activities and that you are entreated to accept as a real person. Annoying as it may be to put up with this ghostly companion, it is best to tolerate her or his presence in your child's life.

Creating an imaginary playmate at this stage in a child's development is a very constructive act. Not every child feels the need to invent such a figure, but those who do are definitely working toward better mental and emotional health.

On a strictly behavioral level, an imaginary playmate is a vehicle your child can use to try out new language and social skills and alleviate loneliness. On a deeper psychological level, an imaginary playmate functions as a valuable projection mechanism for different "selves" within your child. As two distinct entities, your child and her or his imaginary playmate can act out the "good" and the "bad" selves within your child's psyche, the "cowardly" and "brave" selves, or the "optimistic" and "pessimistic" selves, and so on. Through this two-part communication, your child can ultimately consolidate different aspects of her or his psyche into one strong personality.

Tolerating the fact that your child has an imaginary play-mate doesn't mean you have to adopt the playmate as another member of your household. Subconsciously, your child is aware that the playmate exists for her or him alone. If you pretend otherwise, you may turn the playmate into a kind of game between you and your child, which not only interferes with the true function of the playmate for the child alone but also increases the potential length of time that the playmate will hang around.

When an imaginary playmate comes to your home, try to follow these guidelines:

■ *Don't deny or make fun of the playmate.*

This will only frustrate and humiliate your child, for whom the playmate definitely has some sort of reality.

■ *Always talk directly to your child instead of to the play-mate.*

This strategy doesn't reject the existence of the playmate, but it does make it clear that you can't see or hear the playmate.

■ *Let the child take all initiatives with the playmate.*

Don't mention the playmate unless your child does and don't take the lead in acknowledging the playmate's existence (e.g., by setting a place for the playmate at the table without being asked to do so).

■ *Cater to the announced presence of the playmate only in a manner that suits you.*

For example, if your child asks you to set another place at the table, you can either do so—assuming it isn't inconvenient—or you can simply ask your child to make other arrangements for the playmate. If your child yells, "Look out! You're going to bump into Sherman!," you can either move or say to your child, "Please tell Sherman he'll have to get out of the way."

■ *Make sure your child always assumes responsibility for the playmate's actions.*

Often a child uses an imaginary playmate as a scapegoat. If your child says, "I didn't do that. Sherman did!" say, "Then tell Sherman that he was wrong and that you will take care of it."

■ *Minimize the need for an imaginary playmate by offer-ing your child alternative companionship.*

The alternative companion might be yourself, a pet, or (with proper permission) your spouse, a sibling, a relative, or a friend (child or adult).

CASE:

Playing It Out

One of the major benefits of play for young children is that it allows them to channel unacceptable behaviors into games. Thus, they simultaneously eliminate a possible catalyst for real-life conflicts and add more fun to their play life.

At age fifteen months, Samantha was an inveterate pincher, poker, and puller. By far her favorite target was her mother. Attempts simply to punish this behavior weren't successful enough. Whenever Samantha pinched or poked her or pulled her hair, her mother would say, "No," and confine her to a playpen for several minutes; but it wasn't long before Samantha pinched, poked, or pulled again. The situation was generating a great deal of emotional stress for Samantha and her mother.

A magazine article about children's play gave Samantha's mother a new idea. Reinterpreting Samantha's behavior as an attempt to "connect" with her mother as well as an age-appropriate drive to exercise her powers of manipulation, Samantha's mother invented a game that might satisfy both purposes. She filled one of her easy-to-open purses with personal items that were small, safe, and expendable. Then, whenever Samantha exhibited the pinch-poke-pull behavior, her mother brought out the purse and gave it to her as a plaything.

As it happened, Samantha delighted in pulling everything out of her mother's purse and then putting everything back in again. Her mother also gave her the purse at other times so that she wouldn't associate it only with pinching, poking, and pulling. Sooner than her mother had thought possible, all pinching, poking, and pulling ceased.

12.

Transitional

Objects

The phrase may be fancy, but what it describes is usually the opposite. A common transitional object for a very young child is a
threadbare blanket, an old stuffed teddy bear, or a bedraggled doll.
It's an item that is especially beloved by the child because it provides
a link to past moments of comfort and security, and so the child relies
on its presence as she or he enters into new experiences. Disconcerted
as many parents are by their two- to six-year-old child's clinging to
a transitional object (especially when the object is ugly), the behavior
itself is a positive sign of courage and resourcefulness.

Very young children exist in a state of ongoing dependence on other
people. A certain degree of fear and disorientation is bound to occur
when circumstances leave them relatively on their own. Such circumstances range from minor shifts in the daily schedule—like playing
without supervision, riding in the car to unknown destinations, or
going to bed at night—to major life-style changes—attending a day-
care center, accepting a new baby into the family, or moving to another
home.

Some children unaccountably take these shifts and changes in
stride. Others respond with unruly behavior or stressful withdrawal.
Those who choose to cope with the assistance of transitional objects
occupy the middle ground. They are learning to control their negative
reactions by reminding themselves of a "core" state of being that will
survive the unsettling experience. This state is symbolized by the
transitional object that the child literally carries from the secure realm
of past experience into the comparatively insecure realm of the immediate or long-range future.

Here are some important points to keep in mind concerning transitional objects:

■ *Don't criticize or tease your child regarding her or his dependence on a transitional object.*

A child who makes use of a transitional object is already trying to manage feelings of incompetence and vulnerability. Your criticism and teasing will simply aggravate these feelings and make your child feel embarrassed or ashamed.

■ *Consider offering your child a transitional object to help her or him manage emotionally trying experiences.*

For example, suppose your child expresses anxiety about going away from home for a family vacation. If a transitional object hasn't already been selected, try suggesting that she or he bring along a favorite toy or object as a special reminder of home.

Another strategy in this situation or a similar one (such as being separated from you for an extended period of time) is to give your child a gift to be used, if desired, as a transitional object. It isn't always necessary for it to have had a long history with the child. A gift coming from you, especially if it is something with which your child has seen you enjoy yourself, can have great symbolic value to her or him.

■ *Avoid encouraging excessive reliance on transitional objects.*

A child can become overwhelmed with toys, stuffed animals, dolls, and other items that are somehow invested—overtly or subtly—with "special" meaning. It's okay to cooperate with your child's choice of transitional objects and to introduce an item as a possible transitional object in times of particular need. However, restrain yourself from routinely encouraging dependence on them. It may influence your child to put too much faith in symbolic support and too little faith in self-reliance.

■ *Don't expect your child to appreciate, or cooperate with, your attempts to take care of the transitional object.*

Your child is likely to balk at having a transitional object cleaned or repaired. It's the sensual qualities that the object has acquired over time—the complex smell, the distinctive texture, the unique appearance—that contribute to its ability to work a reassuring magic. Your child probably won't even want you to notice or handle the object very much. After all, it represents something very personal and private to him or her.

Of course, if your child is distressed about the damaged condition of the object, you should certainly offer to repair or replace it. To ensure that all goes well, let your child be involved in the repair or replacement.

■ *When it does become necessary to wean your child away from a transitional object, do so gradually and tactfully.*

As your child becomes older, she or he may continue to keep a particular transitional object close at hand merely out of habit or sentimentality. While it's difficult to judge the precise time when your child has outgrown a genuine need for this object, you can intervene to start weaning your child away from it when you think such action is appropriate.

Avoid just taking the object away, whether or not your child is present. Instead, try to interest your child in something else. For example, if she or he clings to the object whenever you travel in the car, try substituting another toy for this purpose or playing a car game to divert attention from the toy.

Also, slowly withdraw your active cooperation in providing your child with this particular object. Don't automatically tell your child to get it when she or he seems out of sorts. Allow it to be forgotten when you leave home. If all else fails, gradually impose limits on its use.

■ *Allow the child to say good-bye to a transitional object in her or his own way.*

When you perceive that your child has ceased to rely on a particular item as a transitional object, don't call attention to the situation by complimenting your child for her or his independence or by engineering the sudden disappearance of the object. Also, leave it to your child to conduct any farewell ceremony (such as burying a disfigured doll or throwing away a hopelessly worn blanket). If your child doesn't take this approach, you shouldn't suggest it.

Just as your child privately elected to transform a certain item into a transitional object, she or he should have the private growth experience of laying it aside in her or his own way and time. Seeing the object still around, stripped of its former importance, can be a valuable reminder to your child of how much—and how successfully—she or he has matured.

Tension Tamers: Sucking and Rocking

A mere generation ago, parents did everything they could to discourage very young children from sucking their thumbs or rocking their heads back and forth. At best, parents considered these habits socially unacceptable and symptoms of possible maladjustment. At worst, they feared that pursuing these habits on a regular basis would cause physical damage. Now thumb sucking, head rocking, and like activities (such as ear clutching, hair twisting, and—sometimes—masturbation) are acknowledged for what they truly are: perfectly normal tension-releasing strategies that may not be pleasant to watch but are nevertheless harmless.

Thumb sucking, the most prevalent form of tension-releasing activity in very young children, can begin right after birth (in fact, it's been observed in the womb). During the first two years, it can occur at any time day or night, although the most popular time appears to be just before sleep, when the child uses it as a natural relaxation technique. After two years, most thumb sucking starts to taper off during the day, except at moments when the child is "compensating" for frustration, tiredness, or hunger. By age six, it all but disappears as other tension releasers (from nail biting and nose picking to vocalizing and playing) take its place.

Head rocking, the next most prevalent tension releaser, typically occurs only in bed and lasts for a much shorter period of time: until around age three, with brief, episodic lapses continuing for several years thereafter. Many infants enjoy banging their head rhythmically (and, thank goodness, softly) against the bars of their crib.

As a general rule, it's wise and safe to tolerate such tension-releasing habits and wait for them to pass as the child matures. Calling negative attention to them will only aggravate the discomfort that's causing the habit in the first place.

Here are some other, more specific guidelines:

■ *If you find that thumb sucking upsets you too much, consider substituting a pacifier for the thumb.*

It's better than unintentionally taking out your irritation on your child. At first, gently remove your child's thumb from her or his mouth while simultaneously inserting the pacifier. After your child has become accustomed to the pacifier rather than the thumb, keep a pacifier handy at all times (or even an open box filled with pacifiers) so that either your child or you can conveniently insert a pacifier when needed. Conversely, if pacifier dependence disturbs you, consider helping your child use her or his thumb instead.

■ *If you're concerned about how strongly your child bangs her or his head against the crib bars, cushion the bars with cardboard.*

Cardboard is much softer than wood, metal, or plastic, but—unlike cloth or foam rubber—it will give your child a similarly satisfying "hard" surface to hit and "hard" noise to hear.

■ *As much as possible, minimize the causes for such tension releasers.*

Try to prevent your child from becoming unduly or overly frustrated, tired, or hungry. Always check out possible reasons *why* your child is crying or experiencing tension *before* leaving her or him to seek release via sucking or rocking. Your child may much prefer to be fed, put to sleep, or simply comforted.

13.
Storytelling

For as long as human beings have enjoyed the power of speech, storytelling—the face-to-face communication of a story—has enabled child and parent to come together and refresh themselves. From the child's point of view, it is a privileged opportunity to observe the parent closely and positively and to develop new understanding, appreciation, and trust. From the parent's point of view, it is an excellent means of recapturing a child's sense of wonder and of expressing care to a child in a nonauthoritarian manner.

As far as a child's emotional life is concerned, storytelling provides consolation, healing, and renewal in a number of unique and far-reaching ways. It gives children potent word pictures and symbols that they can use to understand and express their feelings. It suggests heroes and role models that they can ponder, imitate, and evaluate. It offers them creative insights into the emotional aspects of human behavior. And it exercises their powers of visual imagination, which is especially beneficial because very young minds often have trouble "seeing" the path into and out of an emotional crisis.

Kids today are immersed in an overtly visual world of television, computers, and video arcades. Even reading aloud to children usually directs them to what they can see on the surface: words and pictures in a book. Person-to-person storytelling stimulates the "mind's eye." The listener has the emotional freedom to envision a story as she or he chooses and the emotional safety of knowing that whatever may be imagined in this context, no matter how frightening, is only "real" in a very temporary, qualified, and experimental sense.

Most important of all, storytelling is compelling in its own right simply because it is fun both for the child and the parent. It associates speaking, listening, and being together with pleasure, and it serves as a "time apart" during the day that defuses troubles and strengthens hope.

Here are some suggestions for making storytelling an especially warm and rewarding activity:

■ *Have confidence in yourself as a storyteller.*

All of us have stories to tell: narratives that we loved as children; anecdotes about our family or circle of friends; plot lines we've picked up from books, television shows, movies, plays, musical comedies, and operas; tales about famous people, places, or events; and accounts of our own daily life. And all of us are capable of sharing stories with others.

If you're shy about storytelling with your child, the secret to confidence lies in preparation. Think in advance of a number of stories you might tell and keep your eyes and ears open for good ones you can borrow. Jot down notes about them to which you can refer from time to time. Practice telling stories to yourself before telling them to your child.

■ *Choose a good time for storytelling.*

The most advantageous circumstance for storytelling is during a regularly scheduled daily storytelling time, one to which you and your child can look forward. When storytelling is an organic part of each day, both of you will participate in it more naturally, with more cooperation and more mental and emotional absorption.

Bedtime is perhaps the most congenial time of all for storytelling. Many children need to achieve an emotional balance at the end of the day before they can fall asleep, and storytelling offers a means of realizing this balance. An alternative to bedtime is just before nap time.

Aside from a regularly scheduled storytelling time, consider telling a story whenever it's relatively quiet around the house and your child needs to be soothed, reassured, or perked up. Storytelling is also an emotionally restorative activity for a child who is sick, away from home, or forced to spend several minutes to a half hour waiting for something.

■ *Create a positive environment for storytelling.*

It's a good idea to establish one particular place in your home as the storytelling spot for non–bedtime stories. Whether or not you establish such a spot, make sure both you and your listener are comfortable and won't be distracted by other people or by outside noises. Dim lighting helps set the mood. Frequent eye contact with your listener will deepen her or his involvement in the story and allow you to gauge how it is being received as you go along.

■ *Give your storytelling session a ritual beginning and ending.*

This cues your listener to accept storytelling as a special event, apart from real-life events. To begin the session, suggest that you both close your eyes while you wait for a story to come to you, light a candle, sing a brief song, or "pluck" a story out of the air with your hands. If you're confident enough about your ability to spin any kind of story, begin by asking your child what kind of story she or he would like to hear. You can also use the same beginning phrase for each story: for example, the traditional "Once upon a time" or something more original like "This is a very special story that I call 'The Story of . . .' "

To end the session, try "reversing" the way you began it. Close your eyes and say good-bye to the story, blow out the candle, sing the brief song again, toss the story back into the air, and/or use a ritual closing line (e.g., ". . . and that is the way the story ends").

■ *Speak in a natural voice, trusting your story to inspire the right language and the right dramatic touches when they are appropriate.*

If you are too stagy when you're telling a story, it may seem forced and lifeless. Try not to speak in a voice that is unnaturally high or thin or in a rhythm that is overly fast or monotonous. And don't worry about whether you're using the right words or giving the story a truly polished recitation. Remember that you're not *performing*; you're *communicating*. You should have just as much fun telling the story as your child has listening to it.

■ *Consider telling a story that has a special bearing on an emotional conflict or crisis your child is experiencing.*

Telling a story can be a very safe and effective way of addressing your child's current emotional difficulties without embarrassing or frightening her or him. After all, a story is an independent entity with a life of its own; and your child remains free to accept it as such or, at her or his discretion, to connect what the story says with what is happening in real life.

When taking this approach to storytelling, be sure that the one you choose depicts a positive resolution. For example, if your child appears to be overcome with sorrow, anger, or guilt, try telling a story in which the hero goes through sorrow, anger, or guilt and emerges in better spirits. If your child seems to be experiencing jealousy or indignation, try one in which these emotions eventually disappear or are reversed rather than one in which the hero merely suffers as a result of these emotions.

Storytelling in general does not always have to involve "happy endings." Indeed, children can gain much wisdom and emotional fortitude from stories that present the unhappy side of life. But at a time when you're fairly certain that your child is wrestling with a particular negative emotion in real life, an upbeat story has a better chance of being consoling.

Choosing Age-Appropriate Stories

BIRTH TO ONE AND A HALF YEARS OLD

Storytelling can begin soon after birth. Although infants typically can't recognize voices and objects until around the ninth month and can't put words together to speak until around the sixteenth month, storytelling helps them become accustomed to the teller's voice and to identify that voice with a peaceful activity.

Storytelling to an infant also lays the groundwork for her or his receptivity to such similar experiences later in life. The infant listener learns to enjoy on a precognitive level the particular rhythmic cadence that inevitably distinguishes a special narrative from everyday chatter. Meanwhile, the teller gets valuable practice in storytelling.

Until your child is around one and a half years old, story content is essentially irrelevant. The act itself is what truly matters. Children this young do seem to appreciate stories that repeat sounds, phrases, and rhythmic patterns (which continues to be true for older children as well).

ONE AND A HALF TO THREE YEARS OLD

Between the ages of one and a half and two years, children typically start speaking on their own. At this point in your child's development, you can begin to form more logical, well-structured stories that enlist your child's understanding and encourage her or his efforts to become more involved in language.

From two to three years old, each child is a little Adam, fiercely bent on labeling everything her or his senses perceive in the immediate surroundings. Stories that name objects, define their function, and associate them with other objects are the most appropriate ones to tell. You can frame such a story by concentrating your attention on a single locale or a single group of items. For example, you may say, "In this room there is a ball, and the ball goes bounce, bounce, bounce. Mommy likes the ball, and the ball is red, and whoops, the ball rolls away. In this room there is also a door . . . ," and so forth. Accompanying the story with some pantomimed hand gestures will keep the listener's attention. Your child may even want to join in when you pantomime.

Stories that build on "What happens next?" are also interesting to children in this age range. Try building a story around what happens, step by step, during one of your own typical days, including the times when you are separated from your child. Be dramatic and imaginative in your rendition of what occurs.

Psychologically, this latter kind of story can be particularly beneficial. It may clear up disturbing mysteries in your child's mind about what goes on in your life. In any event, it reassures your child that when you do go away, you still think about her or him—and that whatever may happen during your day, you do ultimately return.

Another option is to spin a yarn about what might happen if the two of you—or just the child—were to go on a walk in the park, visit Grandmother, or perform some other fairly familiar activity. This helps your child be better prepared, intellectually and emotionally, when such experiences actually take place in the future.

THREE TO FOUR AND A HALF YEARS OLD

Newly capable of identifying some of the more basic emotions and of articulating major likes and dislikes, three-year-old children develop feelings of great intensity. They form very specific images in their minds and hearts of what they want and take the initiative in seeking out situations that have the potential of bringing them love, pleasure, and comfort.

You can now begin to weave more conventional story plots, keeping the narrative flow of events simple, active, and direct. "Goldilocks and the Three Bears" is an excellent example of such a story. It reflects a young child's search for "just the right thing" and, in addition, the child's recognition that things come in different sizes, including people.

Ordinary items that fascinate children of two to five years (and alternately inspire fear and attraction) include holes, puddles, cars, planes, trucks, birds, dogs, cats, squirrels, rain, snow, thunder, lightning, houses, shops, meals, and snacks. Story subjects that interest children in this age range tend to be extraordinary variations on these items: animals that behave like humans, weather that is particularly strong or magical, and so forth. An especially compelling story is one in which the hero (a reflection of the listener) is able to manipulate her or his environment in some wondrous way.

FOUR AND A HALF TO SIX YEARS OLD

Children in this age range are beginning to develop self-consciousness. As they interact more with other children and adults and venture more often away from home base, they become increasingly concerned with personality, social, and sexual differences. One major product of this concern is a new complication in their relationship with their parents: Sons tend to perceive their father as a rival for their mother's romantic interest, and daughters tend to regard their mother as a rival for their father's romantic interest.

Dealing emotionally with this perception as well as with their dawning recognition of adult-world problems like divorce, poverty, crime, and violence, children within this age range become passionately concerned about justice. The questions uppermost in their minds are How can this happen? Is it fair? Will I get what I deserve? Will others get what they deserve? How can things work out for the best?

This is the golden age range for classic fairy tales and folktales, which typically depict an individual triumphing over difficulties to gain fame, wealth, or romance and to restore moral order. The individual may be a princess (Snow White), a puppet (Pinocchio), or a pet (Puss-in-Boots). The difficulties may include a misfortune (the expulsion from an improverished home that Hansel and Gretel suffer), a malefactor (the sorceress who turns the prince into a frog), or a monster (the giant who lives at the top of Jack's beanstalk). Whatever the combination—retold or invented—the listener is provided with a "play" world within which she or he can mentally recast dramas from her or his own newly complex emotional life.

Suggestions for Reading Aloud

Reading stories aloud doesn't provide the emotional intimacy and creativity that face-to-face storytelling does, but it still serves many of the same therapeutic functions. In addition, it helps to acquaint children with the world of books, which can offer valuable private experiences of emotional release and consolation later in the child's life.

Listed below are suggested stories to read aloud that can assist a child in managing major emotional issues or situations occurring between the ages of two and a half and six. Your local librarian can make other recommendations.

Anger at Own Helplessness

Sara and the Door, Virginia A. Jensen (Reading, Mass.: Addison-Wesley, 1977). Ages two and a half.
Leo the Late Bloomer, Robert Kraus (New York: Scholastic, 1981). Ages four to six.

Anger at Parent

Daddy Is a Monster . . . Sometimes, John Steptoe (Philadelphia: Lippincott, 1980). Ages four to six.

Depression

Today Was a Terrible Day, Patricia R. Giff (New York: Viking, 1980). Ages four to six.

Jealousy Regarding a New Baby

Alex and the Baby, Mary Dickinsin (New York: Andre Deutsch, 1982). Ages three to six.
Nobody Asked Me If I Wanted a Baby Sister, M. Alexander (New York: Dial, 1971). Ages three to six.
That New Baby, S. Stein (New York: Walker, 1974). Ages three to six.

Jealousy Regarding a Peer

Jealousy, Eva Eriksson (New York: Carolrhoda, 1985). Ages three to six.

Sibling Conflicts

Sisters, David McPhail (New York: Harcourt, 1984). Ages three to six.

Separation Anxiety

First Pink Light, Eloise Greenfield (New York: Crowell, 1976). Ages three to six.

Divorce

Dinosaurs Divorce: A Guide for Changing Families, Laurene K. Brown and Marc Brown (Boston: Atlantic Monthly, 1986). Ages three to six.

Loneliness

Dear Phoebe, Sue Alexander (Boston: Little, Brown, 1984). Ages three to six.

Shyness

Fiona's Bee, Beverly Keller (New York: Coward-McCann, 1975). Ages four to six.

Hatred

The Hating Book, Charlotte Zolotow (New York: Harper, 1969). Ages four to six.

Toilet Training

Once Upon a Potty, Alona Frankel (New York: Barron's, 1980). Ages two to four (*note*: male and female versions available).

Death

The Dead Bird, M. W. Brown (New York: Dell, 1980). Ages two to four.
Pop's Secret, M. Townsend and R. Stern (Reading, Mass.: Addison-Wesley, 1980). Ages three to six.

Fear (General)

The Red Lion, Diane Wolkstein (New York: Crowell-Collier, 1977). Ages four to six.

Fear of Dogs

The Biggest, Meanest, Ugliest Dog in the Whole Wide World, Rebecca Jones (New York: Macmillan, 1982). Ages three to six.

Fear of Storms

Thunderstorm, Mary Szilagyi (New York: Bradbury Press, 1985). Ages three to six.

Nightmares

No Elephants Allowed, Deborah Robison (Boston: Houghton Mifflin, 1981). Ages three to six.

14.
Day Care

In just twenty-five years, day care has become a necessity for millions of American children. According to the most recent Census Bureau estimates (1988), over half of the kids now under five years old have working mothers and are dependent for care on nonrelatives during the day, compared with less than 30 percent in 1970. And while only 15 percent of such kids received day-care services in 1970, today almost 40 percent do: 15 percent in day-care centers and 24 percent in private homes (so called family-based day care).

These figures are almost certain to grow higher in the years to come as more and more women have no choice but to work. The same Census Bureau estimates reveal that two-thirds of all working women today—as opposed to one-third in 1970—are either the sole support of their family or have husbands who earn less than $15,000.

Given this trend, the main question regarding day care is no longer what it was in 1970—"Should I send my child to day care?" Now that day care has evolved into an unavoidable fact of life for so many Americans, the main question is "What effect will day care have on my child's emotional health?"

So far, experts have been unable to establish definitive answers to this question. The few authoritative follow-up tests that have been conducted on day-care children suggest that day care *in itself* is not noticeably positive or negative in its overall impact on the child's emotional health. Much more important, and ultimately decisive, is the relationship between parent and child, regardless of whether or not the child is in day care.

At the same time you are planning to send your child to day care, you should also plan to arrange your schedule so that the two of you will have especially close, joyful, and dependable periods of time together each day, however brief they may be. This will help ensure that you remain emotionally in tune with each other and that any problems that your child may be having—whether or not they involve day care—won't go unnoticed.

In addition, you should shop around for the best possible day-care service in your price range; and after you've enrolled your child in a day-care service, you should monitor her or his day-care life to make sure it is satisfactory. While tests may show that day care *in itself* has no discernible effect on a child's emotional well-being, these same tests also indicate that the *quality* of a specific day-care facility can make a significant difference.

Here are some steps you should take in choosing and monitoring a day-care service:

■ *Familiarize yourself with state regulations concerning day care.*

Regrettably, there are no federal laws governing the care of small children. Instead, each state has its own regulations. Some have very strict licensing qualifications and procedures; others don't. Make sure any day-care service you're interviewing—or using—complies with the regulations in your state.

■ *Generate a large list of different kinds of day-care centers to visit.*

Comparison shopping makes for a better fit between child and service. Seek information on day-care centers as well as family-based day care. Besides recommendations from relatives and friends, check other sources, such as parent organizations, community service groups, and child welfare agencies.

Also, continue to keep your eyes and ears open for good-quality day-care centers and family-based day care even *after* you've enrolled your child in a particular service. You never know when you may have to change.

■ *Ask about staff members' education, training, experience, and commitment.*

Some day-care services or staff members may be well qualified only to care for children in a particular age range—for example, three to five instead of one to three. Also, turnover is a big problem in day-care services. Other considerations aside, your child will be more emotionally secure at a day-care service if the staff has had a long-term history there and remains constant during your child's day-care life. Find out how long staff members have been at the service and how long they intend to stay.

■ *Ask about the ratio of children to staff member.*

Good children-to-staff-member ratios are no more than four to one for infants under eighteen months old; five to one for children eighteen months to two years; eight to one for children two to three years; ten to one for children three to four years; and fifteen to one for children four to six years. Only a few states mandate ratios in these ranges. Some states allow up to twelve children of any age per staff member.

No matter what the ratios, your child will probably receive more emotionally satisfying individual attention in a service with a small number of children than in one with a large number of children. This means that a ratio of ten children to two staff members is preferable to a ratio of twenty children to four staff members.

■*Ask about their resources and daily program of activities.*
Make sure that your child will have plenty of opportunities for play and rest, a variety of playthings in good condition, and ample space to roam indoors and outdoors.

■*Ask about policies and procedures regarding discipline, safety, sickness, and visitation.*
Policies and procedures regarding discipline should be harmonious with those you have at home. The facilities should be fully "childproof" and hygienic. Parents should be free to visit the service at any time during the hours it is open.

■*Ask for references.*
Get the names and addresses or phone numbers of at least three families who relied on the service for an extensive period of time. Be sure to follow up on these references and to discuss any complaints you hear with the service itself.

■ *Observe the day-care facility and personnel at work before you enroll your child.*
Check for the following:

■ How competent are staff members in dealing with children of different ages and temperaments?

■ How effective are staff members in giving care and encouragement to each individual child?

■ Do the various activities during the day seem well scheduled, well planned, and well run?

■ Do the children seem to like the staff members?

■ How safe and clean is the facility?

■ Is there plenty of well-equipped space for different types of individual and group activities?

■ How safely and effectively do staff members handle crises, such as illnesses, injuries, or emergency situations?

■ How hygienically and efficiently do they change diapers? Illnesses commonly spread from one child to another in day care due to staff members not washing their hands or the station between changes.

■ *Visit the day-care facility from time to time while your child is in its care.*

Periodic firsthand observation for at least an hour each visit is the best way to tell if your child remains emotionally well adjusted to day-care life as time goes by. Try to be discreet during your visit, allowing staff members and your child to go about their usual routines without interference.

■ *Investigate possible sources for any unhappiness you or your child may have about the day-care service.*

It's better to be overly cautious than lax in this regard, for your own peace of mind, for your child's, and for the reputation of the service itself.

■ *Don't hesitate to change day-care services if you feel yours is unsatisfactory.*

Very young children are emotionally resilient enough to handle a switch in day-care services with little trouble, and it's much better to switch than to leave a child in a service that you don't wholeheartedly like.

Early Education: Yes or No?

As distinct from nursery schools, do academically enriched programs for preschoolers give them a head start toward scholastic success in life? Research to date offers no evidence that they do and suggests that an educationally enriched home life provides all the intellectual stimulation a very young child needs or can handle.

Children under six learn better through the type of spontaneous activity associated with play than they do through the controlled, pressurized format of adult-driven learning programs. The major reason has to do with brain development.

While many children under six may be capable of the type of rote learning required for performing simple math calculations and even reading words, most children in this age range still have a couple of years to go before they've developed the physical brain-cell connections necessary for the cognitive skills that underlie lasting academic intelligence. Among these skills are recognizing patterns, envisioning spaces, and sustaining an attention span. As a result, any academic gains that are made by a three- or four-year-old tend to be lost by the time the child is six, by which time "unschooled" peers can quickly catch up.

Another reason why children do not seem to benefit from preschool learning has to do with their emotional makeup. Expert observers have concluded that while very young children in academically enriched programs can derive personal satisfaction from pleasing their parents with what they've learned, they are also prone to be more anxious, less creative, and less positive toward "schooling" in general than children who are not in such programs.

Added to these potential problems is the often overlooked risk of failure. Children under six do not take losing well, and academically enriched programs inevitably set up standards that some children simply may not be able to achieve—or may not be able to reach at a desired rate. Such an inability to meet expectations can have a negative impact not only on the child's feelings but also on those of the parents, try as the latter might to be indifferent and accepting no matter how their child performs.

For all the disclaimers about the effectiveness or value of preschool educational programs, more testing still needs to be done before we can dismiss preschool education entirely. However, we do know enough now to say that parents should not assume that such programs are necessary in order for their child to live up to her or his intellectual potential, nor should parents push their child to cooperate with such programs if she or he seems resistant.

Other points to consider about preschool education are as follows:

■ *Guard against imposing your personal values and ambitions on your child.*

Granted, it's often very difficult to draw a line between what you would want for yourself and what is best for your child. Nevertheless, as far as academic matters go, try as much as possible to follow your child's lead.

First see what your child is *naturally* interested in doing or learning, then experiment with different ways to cultivate those interests. Being too quick to steer your child toward certain preconceived areas of—and approaches toward—learning may prevent you and your child from realizing her or his most promising talents.

■ *Expose your child to a variety of intellectually stimulating toys, resources, and activities.*

The very best things you can do at home to increase your child's love of knowledge are to read to, tell stories to, and talk seriously with your child about subjects that interest her or him. Also, treat your child frequently to short, educationally enriching excursions outside the home: for example, to a nature preserve, a science museum, a zoo, or a factory.

■ *Give your child many opportunities to interact with other people, including adults as well as children.*

Researchers have found that children attending preschool educational programs do seem to have better social skills than those who do not. In fact, some experts feel that the sheer interactivity among children, their peers, and their adult teachers that is built into these programs fuels a great deal of the learning that occurs.

There are a number of ways that you can provide your child with similarly interactive experiences. Attending a day-care service will give her or him a certain amount of exposure to other children and adults; but there are other measures you should consider instead of, or in addition to, day care. Set up regular times for your child to play with other children. Encourage your friends and relatives to spend time with your child. Include your child in your own group activities whenever appropriate.

When your child is three and a half to five years old and fairly mature in social situations, consider enrollment in a nursery school, which concentrates on developing a very young child's play and social skills. To choose a good nursery school for your child, follow the same basic procedures recommended here for choosing a good day-care center.

CASE:

"So Help Me, Harry!"

Jeff's son (now eight years old) had experienced several difficult weeks making the transition to day care: crying each

morning before it was time to leave, clinging to whichever
parent drove him to the day-care center, and acting withdrawn
and resentful the first hour that he was back at home. After
several visits to the center and interviews with staff members,
Jeff had determined that the problem was separation anxiety.

To help make sure that his three-year-old daughter, Crystal,
did not suffer as badly, Jeff decided to begin acclimating Crystal to the upcoming change in her routine about a month in
advance. Gradually, day by day, Crystal spent more and more
time with a baby-sitter. After two weeks, Jeff introduced a new
ritual: telling a story to Crystal just before it was time for her
to be with the baby-sitter. The very first story he told can be
summarized as follows:

*A little girl went out into the yard and found a beautiful little
doll. After playing with the doll for a while and making it smile
and laugh, she noticed that the doll was crying. The doll admitted that she belonged to another little girl who had lost her
and that she didn't know how to get back home. The little girl
said what her mother [like Crystal's mother] always said when
she was stumped: "So help me, Harry!" All at once, a magical
elf named Harry appeared and told the little girl who owned
the doll and how to get in touch with this person.*

Thereafter, the stories that Jeff told Crystal at this particular time of the day were always about Harry coming to help
the little girl in various ways. Not only did these storytelling
sessions enable Jeff and Crystal to enjoy each other's company
just before a temporary separation, but also the running theme
of the stories subconsciously gave Crystal confidence that she
could call on her own "special power" to help her meet special
challenges. By the time day care began, Crystal was used to
being separated from her father, plus she actually looked forward to leaving home because that stage of the day began with
a "So Help Me, Harry!" story.

15.

Psychotherapy

When children under six years old are going through a sustained period of moodiness or troublesome behavior, worried parents typically take solace in this favorite piece of popular wisdom on the subject: "Ignore it! The kid will outgrow it!" These words not only hold out hope; they also cater to the parents' instinctive and understandable wish to deny that their children might be seriously disturbed.

Sometimes this "ignore" policy turns out to be harmless. From birth to age six, children are developing so rapidly in every regard—physically and emotionally, intellectually and spiritually, socially and personally—that a certain number of transient, "phase-related" problems are inevitable.

In many cases, however, this policy runs counter to the best interests of the child or the family. Unfortunately, only time will tell whether ignoring a given problem is harmless or harmful.

Far better advice for parents is *never* to ignore a child's emotional difficulties, regardless of how young she or he may be. At the very least, a parent faced with such difficulties should be *extra* vigilant. On the one hand, the alert parent may get an unexpected opportunity to help the child resolve her or his problems in the quickest and most constructive manner. On the other hand, those problems may get much worse, either so suddenly that only an alert parent will be able to respond in time or so gradually that only an alert parent will be able to tell that it's happening.

In addition to being extra vigilant whenever a very young child is going through emotional difficulties, a parent should be ever mindful of her or his powers and limitations as far as child rearing is concerned. All on their own, parents can make an enormous, positive difference in how their very young children cope emotionally with the stresses and strains of daily life as well as with the pressures and pains of self-development. But there may come times when even the most competent parents are unable to read a child's distress signals, assist a child in overcoming her or his problems, or change a family situation that is causing or aggravating a child's problems. When these times come, parents shouldn't hesitate to seek professional help.

Parents commonly appreciate the fact that any emotional turmoil experienced by a very young child is also likely to affect the family as a whole. They have a much more difficult time accepting the possibility that their own personal problems as parents may actually be fueling that emotional turmoil in the first place. Mixed feelings of pride, shame, hope, fear, responsibility, and guilt interfere with this type of self-knowledge.

Parenting a very young child is one of the most challenging tasks an individual, or a couple, can undertake. First-time parents may find that the transition from an adult-oriented home life to a child-oriented home life is far more complicated and traumatic than they could ever have anticipated. Parents who already have children may have trouble balancing all the new demands on their time and attention while still preserving space for themselves, their marriage, and their other children.

And then there is the issue of the parent's personality versus the child's personality. Frequently, parents are doing all the "right" things, the child is developing "normally," and their life together is free of any "typical" cause for emotional disturbance. Nevertheless, the child's behavior clearly indicates distress. In such cases, the real problem may simply be a poor fit between the personality of the child and that of the parent. This possibility easily gets overlooked by parents of very young children, who erroneously assume that parent-child personality clashes can occur only when a child is older and more independent.

Parents must always keep in mind that a child has a very distinct personality from birth onward and that it may not be automatically compatible with the personalities of her or his parents. An unusually bold child may be confronted with an unusually cautious mother. A very playful father may be surprised by a very serious child. An exceptionally reserved couple may wind up with an exceptionally demonstrative child. Thus, both first-time and experienced parents may discover that a child presents them with specific, personality-related problems in addition to the general problems associated with parenting.

In any of these problematic parenting scenarios, the result can be doubts, resentments, anxieties, and frustrations that may easily lead to troublesome complications. Parents may unwittingly develop an overall child-rearing style that's inappropriately intense, casual, or erratic. Open conflicts may frequently break out between parent and child or between parent and parent.

Ultimately, as the parent-child relationship or the parent-parent relationship continues to be stressful, one or both of the parents may succumb to parental "burnout." Characterized by physical and emotional depression, parental burnout often leads to an involuntary carelessness that subtly undermines the psychological health of every individual in the family.

Just as it's perfectly normal for parents of very young children to have these problems, it should also be appropriate for parents experiencing such problems to consult a child psychologist, a child psychiatrist, or a social worker specializing in child and family psychotherapy. Such an individual is well qualified to assist both parents and children within a family in working through the causes and effects of their emotional problems.

Diagnostic techniques and treatments involving children under six years old vary considerably according to the specific situation. When the child is too young to talk, parental interviews are especially important. Parents are asked about their perceptions of their child and about their relationship with their child and with other family members, including their own parents.

To get a more intimate picture of how parents interact with their nonspeaking child, doctors or therapists also usually observe the parents playing with the child, bathing the child, feeding the child, and/or changing the child's diapers. Often doctors or therapists play with the child themselves to test how she or he responds to a stranger and to a variety of stimuli (such as different voices, expressions, and games). If it appears possible that a physical condition may be responsible for the child's behavior, then relevant medical tests are recommended.

When the child is old enough to talk, doctors and therapists often try "play therapy" in addition to age-appropriate variations of the procedures already mentioned. In play therapy, a child acts out emotions and discusses concerns in the contest of playing with dolls, toys, and games provided by the doctor or therapist.

Play therapy's indirect approach to eliciting a child's feelings and experiences avoids some of the problems that can arise in directly interviewing someone this young. Potential problems of this nature include the chance that the questions themselves might "lead" the responses; the risk that the child might be frightened by the dialogue; and the possibility that the child's replies might be inaccurate because of comprehension or communication difficulties or the child's wish to conceal the truth due to fear, guilt, or a desire to please.

Whatever complications may be involved in psychotherapy for a child under six, it is well worth considering if you are at an impasse in understanding or managing an emotional problem that your child has been exhibiting for several weeks on a fairly persistent basis. Many of the emotional problems that torment an individual at a later age have their origin in the early years of life. If these problems had been addressed when they were still in their initial stage of development, then years of needless suffering might have been avoided.

Here are some issues to consider in finding the right doctor or therapist for you, your child, and your family:

---

1. Before you begin your search, establish what you consider to be the problem you want addressed and the goal you want achieved.

First, write down your answers to the following five questions, bearing in mind that some of your answers may overlap.

a. What specific behaviors have I observed indicating that my child may be experiencing emotional turmoil? (To whatever extent possible, give dates, times of day, settings, and circumstantial surroundings.)

b. How would I define this emotional turmoil? (In other words, if you had to make a diagnosis, what would it be?)

c. What might be the cause(s) of this turmoil? (Include any speculations as well as any more conclusive opinions you may have—being careful to distinguish between these two categories.)

d. In what different ways has this emotional turmoil been bothersome or detrimental to my child, to me, and to other members of the family? (Be as specific as possible, as you were directed in answering question a.)

e. How have I tried to better the situation? (Indicate which methods have been at least partially successful and which have failed altogether).

Once you have answered all five questions to the best of your ability, write down a fairly succinct (one- or two-sentence) description of what you think the *problem* is. Next, write an equally succinct description of the *goal* that you want to achieve related to this problem: that is, what you would like to see happen *as a result* of psychotherapeutic intervention.

These statements, as well as the question-and-answer background material, will be enormously helpful to you in interviewing possible doctors or therapists. They will also be enormously helpful to the doctor or therapist you choose in her or his efforts to diagnose and treat your child successfully.

2. *Familiarize yourself with the major types of therapy that are available.*

The sheer variety of therapy labels is bewildering to the outsider: psychoanalytic (Freudian, Jungian, Adlerian, or otherwise), cognitive, behavioral, existential, Gestalt, transactional, reality-oriented, rational-emotive, and so on. However, for the purpose of interviewing potential doctors or therapists to work with a child under six years old, all you need is a very basic awareness of three broad categories of psychotherapy: psychodynamic therapy, behavioral therapy, and family-oriented therapy.

■ *Psychodynamic therapy* is geared toward getting the child to identify, understand, and self-manage her or his emotional problems. Because it depends heavily on effective verbal communication between the doctor or therapist and the child, it is not appropriate for children who have not begun to speak fairly fluently. (Usually this means children under four years old.) It also tends to be relatively long-term compared to the other categories of psychotherapy, often involving multiple sessions per week for up to a year or two.

■ *Behavioral therapy* is geared toward getting the child to change the way she or he behaves. Instead of focusing squarely on the causes of a particular problem, it concentrates on the symptoms. For example, it might help children learn to control their anger without necessarily getting them to appreciate why they get angry, to be less scared of nightmares regardless of whether they know about their possible source, or to interact more cooperatively with other people even if their feelings about them remain unresolved. It typically takes at least a few months of weekly or biweekly sessions before satisfactory results can be expected.

■ *Family-oriented therapy*, sometimes known as "systems therapy," is one of the types of therapy practiced at Philadelphia Child Guidance Center (PCGC) and the type that PCGC recommends most highly for children of any age, but especially for children under six years old. Drawing upon both psychodynamic therapy and behavioral therapy, family-oriented therapy is geared toward generating positive awareness and change in all aspects of the child's world: her or his own mind and behavior as well as the minds and behaviors of those people who directly influence her or his life. In comparison to the other therapies, it is much more adaptable to the situation at hand. Satisfactory results may be achieved in just one or two sessions or may take up to a year or two.

Use these very basic distinctions as beginning points for discussing with other people (such as knowledgeable advisers and potential doctors or therapists) the particular type or types of psychotherapy that may be appropriate to your unique situation. Also, investigate the literature about child psychotherapy that's available at local libraries and bookstores. The more informed you are about it—whatever form it may take—the more benefit you'll derive from the type of psychotherapy you finally choose, whatever it may be.

3. *Familiarize yourself with the major types of doctors and therapists that are available.*

The three most common practitioners of child-oriented psychotherapy are psychiatrists, psychologists, and social workers. Regardless of the specific title (e.g., "psychiatrist"), not all of these practitioners have special training or experience in treating children in particular as opposed to people in general. This is an important issue that you will want to investigate with individual practitioners that you interview.

Also, keep in mind that one type of practitioner, all else being equal, is not necessarily more or less desirable than another. Your final determination should be based on how appropriate the individual practitioner is, given the following factors: your child's problem, the goals you've established relating to that problem, the type of therapy you're interested in pursuing, your financial resources, and most important of all, the overall personalities of you and your child.

These warnings having been given, here are brief descriptions of each major type of practitioner:

■ *Psychiatrists* are medical doctors (M.D.s), which means that they have had four years of medical school, one year of internship, and at least two years of residency training in psychiatry. In addition, virtually all child psychiatrists have had two-year fellowships in child psychiatry and are board certified.

One major advantage of a psychiatrist over other types of practitioners is that she or he can diagnose and prescribe treatment for physical problems that may be causing or aggravating a child's emotional problems. A possible disadvantage, depending on your particular situation, is that some psychiatrists (usually not *child* psychiatrists) are inclined to practice only psychodynamic forms of therapy.

■ *Psychologists* have usually earned a doctorate (Ph.D.) in psychology, typically the result of five years of graduate training, including several supervised clinical programs and a year of formal internship. Most states also require postdoctoral experience before licensing. Some states, however, require only a master's degree (M.A.) to become a psychologist.

Although psychologists themselves cannot offer physical diagnosis and prescription, they almost always have close professional relationships with physicians whom they can recommend for such services. They are also likely to be more eclectic in their therapeutic style, although there is still a trend among psychologists to favor behavioral therapy.

■ *Social workers* have earned a master's degree in social work (M.S.W.), a process that involves two years of classes and fieldwork. In addition, some states require two or more years of postgraduate experience before licensing.

While social workers may not have had the extensive academic and clinical training that psychiatrists and psychologists have had, they are, as a rule, much more familiar with—and knowledgeable about— the home, community, and school environments of their clients. This background inclines them to practice family-oriented or systems-oriented therapy more than other types of therapy.

Another major issue to consider in choosing a particular type of doctor or therapist is whether the therapy will occur in a *private office* or a *clinic*. Other factors aside, therapy performed in clinics tends to be more multidimensional: a by-product of the fact that clinics are so often staffed with various types of doctors and therapists, who not only practice different kinds of therapy but also conduct different kinds of research projects.

---

4. Make a rough estimate of how much you can afford to spend on your child's therapy.

It may be impossible to put a price on a child's emotional well-being. However, it's quite possible to determine how much you can afford to spend for psychotherapy without making life much more difficult for yourself and your family—a situation that could only exacerbate your child's emotional problems.

You may have insurance that will cover some or all of the expenses directly incurred as a result of your child's therapy; but in the best of situations there are bound to be some hidden costs. Factor into your budget such possibilities as lost income for days off work, transportation and parking for therapy sessions, and baby-sitting care for other children while you are at the sessions.

In estimating how much you can afford for the therapy itself, take into account that private therapy is almost certain to be more expensive than therapy in a clinic. Also, clinics may offer lower fees if you accept therapy from a supervised student therapist or agree to participate in a research project (which typically means being observed, taped, and/or interviewed).

5. Seek several recommendations from a variety of qualified sources.

Ask relatives and friends who have benefited from the services of child psychiatrists, psychologists, or social workers for their opinions, but also seek leads from more experienced and disinterested parties, such as your pediatrician, family physician, and clergyperson. For the names of certified practitioners in your area, contact local and national mental-health and professional organizations (see Appendix for a list of suggestions).

6. Interview different doctors and therapists thoroughly about their credentials, areas of expertise, and therapeutic techniques.

Among the specific questions you should ask are the following:

■ What is your educational and training background (see issue 3)?

■ Are you board certified? By whom?

■ With what professional organizations are you affiliated (see Appendix for a list)?

■ How long have you practiced in your current capacity?

■ What is your general or preferred style of therapy (see issue 2)?

■ What are your areas of special expertise?

■ How much work have you done with children who are the same age as my child?

■ How much work have you done with the type of problem(s) my child is having (see issue 1)?

■ Would you feel committed to achieving the goal I have in mind (see issue 1)?

■ What kinds of services can I expect from you toward meeting this goal?

■ What kinds of commitment and cooperation would you expect from me and my family in the course of my child's therapy?

■ How, and at what rate, will you keep me informed of the progress my child is making in therapy?

■ How much time do you estimate the therapy might take?

■ How much will it cost, will my insurance or medical assistance help pay the cost, and are there ways to reduce the cost (see issue 4)?

7. *Make sure that you choose a doctor or therapist who respects you and with whom you are comfortable.*

Some doctors or therapists may unintentionally cause you to feel guilty or incompetent, in which case you should look for someone else. The doctor or therapist you select should be a person who inspires you to feel good about yourself: *re*moralized instead of *de*moralized.

Your answer to each of the following questions should be yes both during your initial interview with a doctor or therapist and throughout the time that the therapy itself is in progress:

■ Does the doctor or therapist take into account *your* theories, opinions, and concerns as well as her or his own?

■ Does the interaction you have with the doctor or therapist seem like a dialogue rather than a monologue on the doctor's or therapist's part?

■ Does the doctor or therapist seem genuinely interested in you and your situation (evidenced by her or his paying close attention to you, maintaining fairly consistent eye contact with you, and regularly soliciting your comments and reactions)?

■ Does the doctor or therapist seem genuinely interested in your child and her or his problems?

■ Does the doctor or therapist make sure that you understand what she or he is doing and saying?

■ Does the doctor or therapist answer all of your questions promptly, thoughtfully, and to the best of her or his ability?

■ Do you leave the doctor's or therapist's company feeling clear about the direction that your child's case will be taking?

■ Do you leave the doctor's or therapist's company feeling generally stronger rather than weaker?

Possible Symptoms of Emotional Problems: Birth to Age Six

BIRTH TO SIX MONTHS

■ failure to put on weight or develop physically within "normal" parameters

■ indifference to feeding

■ poor eye contact and indifference to human voice and play

■ persistent sleep disturbance (apart from colic-related sleep loss or simply not sleeping through the night)

■ hypersensitivity to sights and sounds

■ ticlike movements of face and hands

■ rumination (swallowing regurgitated foods)

SIX MONTHS TO ONE YEAR

■ persistent self-injurious behavior (other than "normal" rocking and head banging)

■ lack of any discernible pattern in sleeping and eating

■ failure to imitate sounds and gestures

■ persistent lack of appropriate emotional response to surprises, fearful situations, or pleasurable stimuli

■ generalized apathy

■ persistent lack of distress when confronted with strangers

■ significant delays in "normal" cognitive and motor development

ONE TO TWO YEARS

■ withdrawn behavior

■ excessive rocking and posturing

■ persistent lack of distress when separated from parents

■ excessive distractibility

- frequent irritability that does not respond to calming efforts (apart from occasional tantrums)

- night wandering

TWO TO THREE YEARS

- persistent fearfulness

- failure to make efforts to talk

- inability to play in any focused manner for ten minutes at a time

- intense and ongoing sibling conflict

- hyperactivity

- persistent and excessive aggressiveness

- slow recovery from angry outbursts

- severe and prolonged reaction to separation from parents

THREE TO SIX YEARS

- frequent incidents of self-punishing or self-injurious behavior

- frequent and severe conflicts with other children

- persistent withdrawal from other children

- general inability to follow rules or directions

- persistent refusal to talk

- sudden, noticeable, and long-lasting declines in general self-confidence, attentiveness, or interest

- persistent depression

Special Diagnoses: Children Under Six

MENTAL RETARDATION

Mental retardation is a very general descriptive term applied to any child who exhibits these two characteristics: (1) an intelligence quotient (IQ) that is *significantly* below normal; (2) *considerable* problems in adapting to everyday life. Retardation in very young children may be complicated by physical problems, such as difficulty in hearing, seeing, or speaking. It may also be complicated by emotional problems, such as ongoing frustration, anxiety, withdrawal, or rebellion. These emotional problems can be associated either with the retarded child's awareness of her or his retardation (most retarded children recognize that they are different from "normal" children) or with her or his general lack of coping abilities.

Mild mental retardation is frequently difficult to diagnose before a child reaches age three, the earliest time at which a reliable IQ test can be administered. In some cases, however, mental retardation is so profound that a diagnosis can be made much sooner. A child may fail completely to reach cognitive, behavioral, and emotional milestones in her or his development, much less to meet them within the "normal" parameters set by experts in child development.

The leading physical cause of mental retardation is *Down syndrome*, a genetic disorder that is also one of the most common birth defects. Today the chance of an American woman's giving birth to a Down child is about 1 in 1,500 when she is under twenty-four, increasing to about 1 in 100 by the time she is forty. Characterized by distinctive facial features—eye folds that make the eyes look slanted, sunken cheekbones, and a protruding tongue—as well as by other physical characteristics, like poor muscle tone, Down syndrome can almost always be diagnosed at birth.

Contrary to popular misconceptions, most mentally retarded children, including children affected by Down syndrome, can learn a great deal, can maintain emotional stability, and, as adults, can lead relatively independent lives. Most important, they can enjoy their lives as much as anyone else. For the most part, they do not require permanent institutionalization; and federal law guarantees them educational as well as other services at public expense.

A very comprehensive evaluation is vital in assessing a retarded child's true developmental and educational potential. Such an evaluation is almost certain to coordinate consultation with a number of different specialists in neurology, hearing, speech, vision, physical therapy, or special education as well as in psychiatry. It's best to perform this evaluation as early in the child's life as possible. The earlier parents know about the very particular nature of their child's retardation, and the earlier they expose their child to intervention programs, the greater the opportunity to effect positive change in her or his physical and emotional well-being.

AUTISM

Autism is a developmental disorder characterized mainly by a child's persistent and severe lack of responsiveness to others as well as severe language problems. The actual cause is unknown. Typically, an autistic child is one who doesn't cuddle, make eye contact, speak, or even make gestures or facial expressions to communicate feelings.

Autism almost always manifests itself within the first three years of a child's life. In addition to the symptoms already mentioned, psychotherapists look for one or more of the following signs:

■ a tendency toward unusual and repetitive movements, such as arm flapping, rigid posturing, stomping, and spinning (older children may develop bizarre and complex rituals associated with bedtime or mealtime);

■ speech oddities, such as persistent "singsong" or monotonous talk;

■ extreme responses to normal occurrences, such as an inconsolable panic reaction to a doorbell ringing;

■ extreme attachment to, or avoidance of, particular objects in the environment, such as a fan, a shoe, or a table;

■ routine self-mutilating behavior, such as cutting oneself with scissors or knives.

Autistic children can usually be helped to lead more "normal" and independent lives with the combination of a more structured environment and proper teaching, training, and motivation. Depending on the particular range of symptoms, sedative or tranquilizing drugs may also be prescribed. Some autistic children can be fully rehabilitated, but many bear some traces of the disorder throughout their lives.

Besides working directly with the autistic child, psychotherapists can help the family as a whole resolve the stress that's commonly associated with having an autistic family member living in the same household. Unlike a child with Down syndrome, who often manifests a happy and loving personality, an autistic child doesn't automatically invite tolerance and compassion. The illness is simply too alien for most people to appreciate. Psychotherapists enable individual family members, regardless of their age, not only to understand autism but also to deal effectively with problem situations the autistic child may create and support her or his progress toward a more emotionally fulfilling life.

ATTENTION-DEFICIT HYPERACTIVITY DISORDER

By far the most common psychiatric disorder of childhood, with an overall prevalence rate of 5 percent, attention-deficit hyperactivity disorder (ADHD) may not be discovered or diagnosed until a child is of school age. At that point, it manifests itself fairly unmistakably as a combination of restlessness, noisiness, an inability to sit still or concentrate, poor socialization, and poor scholastic performance. Nevertheless, the disorder has its roots in much earlier stages of a child's development. In fact, one of the commonly accepted criteria for a professional diagnosis of ADHD is that there must have been indications of the disorder *prior* to school age.

The causes of ADHD are generally biochemical in nature. In infants and toddlers, ADHD manifests itself in excessive crying, sleeping problems, feeding difficulties, and a host of other "troublesome behaviors," including, possibly, colic. In children from three to six years old, it usually shows up as excessive motor activity, difficulty paying attention or listening, aggressiveness, and an extremely short attention span.

Psychotherapists who suspect ADHD from a very young child's history will recommend a medical evaluation to determine if there may be some alternative explanation for her or his symptoms: for example, a hearing impairment, hyperthyroidism, a seizure-related condition, or an allergy. If ADHD does seem to be the source of the child's problems, then the psychotherapist helps the child and the family develop coping strategies—for example, procedures that will keep the child focused on individual tasks as they present themselves and help the child pace her- or himself through the performance of each task in an appropriate manner. In cases in which a diagnosis of ADHD is indisputable, medication may also be prescribed.

At PCGC: Preschool At-Risk Program

Families in which there is a history of mental illness, substance abuse, or child abuse often require special assistance. Parents need to develop better parenting skills through building their level of confidence and comfort in dealing with their children. Children need to receive the particular care and education that will enable them to overcome their problems and live more competent lives.

PCGC's Preschool At-Risk Program helps families who fall into the above-mentioned "at risk" categories. Children in the program are drawn from the preschool population and are referred to the program by teachers and caretakers as well as by the Social Work Department of The Children's Hospital of Philadelphia and the Child Development Department of Children's Seashore House.

Specifically, the program offers the following services:

EVALUATIONS

Each child is given a psychoeducational assessment to determine levels of functioning, and home visits are conducted to assess how well the family functions. From these assessments, an individual program plan is developed. If appropriate, other, more specialized assessments are performed by psychologists, psychiatrists, and/or speech therapists.

CLASSROOM WORK

The work in the program's special classroom format involves the family as a whole and integrates family therapy with educational activities. The three main objectives of the classroom approach are as follows:

1. to create learning tasks that are relevant to the child's developmental level, parental concerns, and issues involving parent-child interactions;

2. to devise successful interpersonal transactions that draw upon and reinforce parental competence;

3. to assist parents in changing their child's behavior and in helping her or him develop cognitive, intellectual, and social skills.

FAMILY THERAPY

This service is provided by a preschool therapist in the program. The therapist meets with families on a weekly basis, either alone, in concert with a psychoeducational therapist, or in the context of the program's classroom.

PARENT SUPPORT GROUP

The parent support group offers an opportunity for parents in the program to come together and discuss general issues related to raising young children as well as specific issues that they are addressing in family therapy or the classroom. By asking questions of one another, sharing experiences, and extending advice, group members come to feel less alienated and more involved in a network of concerned parents. The result is a living, evolving resource that any member can tap: for personal relief, for crisis-related information, for baby-sitting, or for family socializing.

Aside from these services, the Preschool At-Risk Program also features several outreach components:

■ A Community Involvement Team (consisting of a psychoeducational specialist and a program therapist) periodically visits families in their home environment. There the team assists families in applying the knowledge they acquired through family therapy and/or the classroom, evaluating the progress they have made in managing difficulties, and identifying any further needs.

■ A model program developed by the Preschool At-Risk Program helps integrate specialized preschool services (e.g., speech therapy) with normal preschool programs, such as Head Start. The effect of this "mainstreaming" is a reduction of the psychologically damaging segregation and isolation that at-risk children with special needs must otherwise endure.

■ The Preschool At-Risk Program coordinates its services with many existing human services agencies and volunteer groups to better serve the parents and children in the program. It also maintains a very strong collaborative relationship with The Children's Hospital of Philadelphia.

If your child, or a child you know, may benefit from a program of this type, consult a local mental-health organization. There may be a similar program in your area.

The Early Years: Selected Terms and Concepts

acting out   indirectly expressing emotional conflicts—or "forbidden feelings"—through negative behavior. Such behavior is typically overdramatic and designed to attract attention. It may or may not be overtly self-punishing or injurious to others. For example, a child who feels rejected by a parent may "act out" that feeling by refusing to speak to that parent, constantly trying to distract the parent, talking back, or picking fights with a sibling who appears to be getting more attention.

affective disorder   also known as *emotional disorder* or *mood disorder*, a specifically defined psychological illness relating to the emotions (e.g., *attention-deficit hyperactivity disorder*). Generally, such a disorder is apparent in the problematic manner in which a child physically displays emotions (hence, the root "affect"). The disorder may also have a physical cause.

attachment   the emotional bond between parent and child. Most often the term is used in reference to the child's bond to the mother, although attachment is a two-way street and also forms between child and father.

Attachment between child and mother is uniquely strong because of the latter's role in childbearing and early caretaking. Conditioned to seek closeness with the mother, the child may suffer emotional difficulties if deprived of maternal affection or if that affection becomes overly demanding.

attention-deficit hyperactivity disorder   an affective disorder involving certain severe and interrelated behavioral problems, such as chronic restlessness, an inability to concentrate or finish tasks, and poor listening skills. In most cases, the disorder is not detected until the child enters school and experiences academic difficulties.

autism a developmental disorder characterized by a persistent and severe lack of responsiveness to others as well as severe language problems.

behavior modeling a therapeutic technique by means of which the child is taught or encouraged to replace negative behaviors with more positive ones. The teaching or encouraging process involves modifying the way that each parent or caretaker interacts with the child so that the child learns by example or direct experience (e.g., a reward system) to behave more constructively.

conduct disorder a psychological problem manifested in chronic, excessively unruly behaviors, such as stealing, running away, lying, or setting fires.

defiance more technically known as *oppositional behavior*, defiance refers to any act on the part of a child that is intentionally designed to challenge parental authority. Common examples include saying no, refusing to perform assigned tasks, and deliberately withdrawing from meals and other prearranged family activities.

distractibility a problematic behavior involving a limited ability to concentrate on a single activity for an appropriate amount of time. Distractibility can be a sign of underlying anxiety, or it can lead to anxiety. It can also be a symptom of *attention-deficit hyperactivity disorder.*

dysfunctional as opposed to *functional*, a term used to describe a personality or family unit that does not operate effectively or satisfactorily to meet day-to-day life challenges. In some cases, there is apparent effectiveness or satisfaction, but achieving it causes underlying psychological damage. In other cases, the personality or family unit is clearly having problems that pose a threat to its survival.

This term is sociological in origin and is rapidly losing currency in the field of psychology. Many therapists consider it too negative and abstract to be useful diagnostically.

emotional disorder (see *affective disorder*)

extroversion a generally outgoing attitude toward the world at large. First defined by Carl Jung, extroversion is also associated with a relatively strong interest in social interactions and concrete realities and a relatively weak interest in self-contained activities and abstract thought.

Extroversion is assumed to be an inborn personality trait that is neither positive nor negative in essence and that can be modified only slightly by experience or conditioning. The opposite quality is *introversion.*

functional   (see *dysfunctional*)

identification   a means of bolstering one's own self-image by associating it with someone else's self-image, either consciously or unconsciously. For a child in the early years, the most common form of identification is with the same-sex parent. However, the object of identification can be anyone—regardless of sex or age—who possesses physical, psychological, or social qualities that the identifier admires or considers absent or deficient in her or his personal identity.

In most cases, the process of identification is a normal and healthy stage in the child's self-development. The form it takes varies according to the individual and may or may not be detectable on the surface. Most often, it involves spending a lot of time around the object of identification, mimicking that person's behavior or extending unqualified devotion and service to that person.

individuation   in the philosophy of Carl Jung, the long process by which a child evolves from being totally dependent on others, emotionally and socially, to being a separate and successful individual with a unique, self-sustaining psychological makeup.

introversion   a generally inward-looking attitude toward the world at large. First defined by Carl Jung, introversion is also associated with a relatively strong interest in self-contained activities and abstract thought and a relatively mild interest in social interactions and concrete realities.

Introversion is assumed to be an inborn personality trait that is neither positive nor negative in essence and that can be modified only slightly by experience or conditioning. The opposite quality is *extroversion.*

maladaptation   also known as *maladjustment*, this term refers to a child's inability to react in a calm, effective, or successful manner either to a single life change or to the demands of life in general.

maladjustment   (see *maladaptation*)

mood disorder　(see *affective disorder*)

oppositional behavior　(see *defiance*)

other-directed behavior　individual actions that are oriented toward other people: for example, seeking attention, initiating and responding to interactions, expressing hostility. Therapists often explore whether a child has a healthy, age-appropriate balance of other-directed behavior and its opposite, *self-directed behavior*.

overanxious disorder　a psychological problem manifesting itself in chronic, generalized, and often irrational feelings of fear, apprehension, and misgiving. There may also be physical symptoms, such as frequent headaches and stomachaches.

overcorrection　a negative effect of the parent-child relationship in which the discipline or punishment imposed on a child's conduct—or the child's "reforming" response to discipline or punishment—exceeds appropriate limits.

phobia　an excessive and persistent fear of particular people, things, or situations. (Precise targets vary from individual to individual.) Phobias are fairly common among children in their early years. Most often they are transitory and not indicative of any serious psychological problem.

projection　an unconscious, self-protecting measure in which a child denies negative, forbidden, or unpleasant feelings and instead attributes them to someone else. In most cases, the person upon whom the child projects such negative feelings is the trigger for them. For example, a child who is angry at Mother may unconsciously reclaim her or his innocence by believing instead that Mother is angry at her or him.

psychopathology　the study of mental illnesses. The term "pathology" refers to a disease or a disorder, as opposed to a less severe problem.

repression　a means of emotional self-protection in which traumatic thoughts or memories are automatically relegated to the unconscious mind and forgotten by the conscious mind. In older children, thoughts or memories that are merely unpleasant may also be repressed, along with traumatic thoughts or memories.

resilience　a child's ability to adapt effectively to change or recover effectively from a crisis. Children that have more resilient emotional natures are likelier to be healthier psychologically.

self-directed behavior   individual actions that are oriented around the self: for example, solitary play or self-punishment. Therapists often explore whether a child has a healthy, age-appropriate balance of self-directed behavior and its opposite, *other-directed behavior*.

temperament   a child's inborn character, which forms the basis of the later-developing personality. Generally speaking, an individual temperament involves a certain combination of behavioral dispositions that can be modified only slightly by later experience. For example, a child may be temperamentally predisposed toward *extroversion* or *introversion*.

"Temperament" is a very loosely defined term. Various schools of psychological thought differ over which emotional characteristics are primarily a matter of temperament, as opposed to being primarily a matter of acquired personality.

withdrawal   a child's willful separation, emotionally or physically, from an event or person that is somehow distressing. In most cases involving very young children, withdrawal is a temporary delaying tactic rather than a more entrenched, long-term, and far-reaching posture. For example, a very young child who is angry with a parent or perceives the parent as being angry with her or him may withdraw from that parent for a while but will quickly abandon such behavior once the feeling or perception passes or is alleviated.

Appendix

Organizations to Contact

I f you believe your child is having serious problems dealing with her or his emotions or behavior, it's a good idea to get a professional evaluation of your child's emotional health and, possibly, professional help for your child. These services should be provided by a well-qualified child psychiatrist, child psychologist, or social worker whom both you and your child like and trust.

To find the professional that's right for your situation, first consult friends and relatives who have had experience with such services, your pediatrician, and your child's school counselor. Also try local organizations, such as medical societies, psychiatric societies, and city, county, and state mental-health associations.

If you are unable to get satisfactory references or locate an acceptable professional using these sources, or if you'd like more background information on the subject and practice of psychotherapy for children, try contacting any of the following organizations for assistance:

American Academy of Child and Adolescent Psychiatry
3615 Wisconsin Avenue, NW
Washington, DC 20016
(800) 222-7636

■ professional society for degreed physicians who have completed an additional five years of residency in child and adolescent psychiatry

■ forty-three regional groups in the United States, equipped to provide information (including consumer guidance on insurance benefits covering child and adolescent psychiatry) and referrals

American Academy of Community Psychiatrists
P.O. Box 5372
Arlington, VA 22205
(703) 237-0823

■ professional society for psychiatrists and psychiatry residents practicing in community mental-health centers or similar programs that provide care regardless of their client's ability to pay

■ seven regional groups in the United States that are equipped to inform the public about a community psychiatrist's training and role and about how to obtain services

American Association of Psychiatric Services for Children
1200-C Scottsville Road, Suite 225
Rochester, NY 14624
(716) 235-6910

■ accrediting service and information clearinghouse for clinics and other institutions offering psychiatric services for children

■ equipped to provide information and referrals

National Association of Social Workers
7981 Eastern Avenue
Silver Spring, MD 20910
(800) 638-8799

■ professional society for people who hold a minimum of a baccalaureate degree in social work (B.S.W.)

■ fifty-five state, district, and protectorate groups that are equipped to inform the public about the services provided by social workers and how to obtain them

American Association for Marriage and Family Therapy
1717 K Street, NW #407
Washington, DC 20006
(202) 429-1825

■ professional society for marriage and family therapists

■ maintains thirty-nine training centers throughout United States that are equipped to provide information and referrals

Psychology Society
100 Beekman Street
New York, NY 10038
(212) 285-1872

■ professional society for psychologists who have a doctorate and are certified/licensed in the state where they practice

■ equipped to provide information and referrals

National Association for the Advancement of Psychoanalysis
and the American Boards for Accreditation and Certification
80 Eighth Avenue, Suite 1210
New York, NY 10011
(212) 741-0515

■ professional society for psychoanalysts that sets standards for training, accredits institutions, certifies individual practitioners, and evaluates institutions and practitioners

■ equipped to offer information and referrals (publishes an annual directory, *National Registry of Psychoanalysts*, with geographic index: $15)

Council for the National Register of Health Service Providers in Psychology
1730 Rhode Island Avenue, NW, Suite 1200
Washington, DC 20036
(202) 833-2377

■ registry for psychologists who are licensed or certified by a state board of examiners of psychology and who have met additional council criteria as health service providers in psychology

■ equipped to provide referrals

National Council of Community Mental Health Centers
12300 Twinbrook Parkway
Rockville, MD 20852

■ membership organization of community mental-health centers

■ not equipped to provide referrals by telephone but publishes a bi-annual *National Registry*, which lists centers by geographic area

Federation of Families for Children's Mental Health
1021 Prince Street
Alexandria, VA 22314
(703) 684-7710

■ organization for parents looking for support and advocacy groups

■ equipped to provide contacts

Index